CHILDREN'S
ENCYCLOPEDIA
OF THE
ENVIRONMENT

ARCTURUS

Picture Credits:
Every attempt has been made to clear copyright. Should there be any inadvertent omission,
please apply to the publisher for rectification.
Key: b–bottom, t–top, c–center, l–left, r–right

Cover insets l-r (anatoliy_gleb), (Svetlana Orusova), (alphaspirit.it), (ohrim), (Parilov), cover main (MEE KO DONG), inside front cover & 12br (Marius Dobilas), inside back cover, 20, 54–55, 92 & 112bl (Riccardo Mayer), back cover & 112–113 (saiko3p), 1 & 42–43 (zhengzaishuru), 4–5 (Emena), 4t (Nok Lek), 4b (Dennis van de Water), 5t (huyangshu), 5c (Photographer RM), 5b (overcrew), 6–7 (Rich Carey), 7t (Maksym_Irkha), 7b (guentermanaus), 8–9 (Stu Porter), 9t (GUDKOV ANDREY), 9b (paula french), 10–11 (Natalia Paklina), 10c (Lorna Roberts), 11t (Martin Prochazkacz), 12–13 & 22–23 (Perfect Lazybones), 13b (Conservationist), 14–15 (Barbara Ash), 14b (Craig Hanson), 15b (ChameleonsEye), 16–17 (COULANGES), 16c (reisegraf.ch), 16b (RLS Photo), 18–19 (worldclassphoto), 18bl (kkaplin), 19bl (Anolis_01), 20–21 & 78–79 (BGStock72), 21t (WAYHOME studio), 22bl (Alex Zabusik), 23t (Tatiana Shepeleva), 24–25 (Grindstone Media Group), 24l (BearFotos), 25r (Wolfgang Jargstorff), 26–27 (Tatjana Baibakova), 27t (Monkey Business Images), 28–29 (Amy Lutz), 28tl (Denis Belitsky), 28br (Charmaine A Harvey), 30–31 (Anna Om), 30cr (Svetlana Foote), 31bl (Arti_Zav), 32–33 (Herschel Hoffmeyer), 32bc (vovan), 33tc (InfinitumProdux), 34–35 (DVKi), 34cr (vvoe), 35cr (John Carnemolla), 36–37 (Mohamad Baihaki), 36bl (yanik88), 37tr (wim claes), 38–39 (Heather Lucia Snow), 38bc (Josef Pittner), 39bl (Tomasz Jocz), 40–41 (industryviews), 41b (Pavel Mikheyev), 42bl (DKai), 43tr (Farknot Architect), 44–45 (solarseven), 44rc (Ziablik), 45bl (VectorMine), 46–47 (Daniel Avram), 46lc (Leonid Sorokin), 47tl & 100 (vchal), 48–49 (RavenEyePhoto), 48rc & 126bl (K_Boonnitrod), 49rc (Vadim Nefedoff), 50–51 (neenawat khenyothaa), 50br (Edson Flores Silloca), 51c & 127tl (Christian Jackson), 52–53 (Ahmad Fachry), 52rc (Harvepino), 53tr (Ververidis Vasilis), 54rc (Artush), 55rc (Kletr), 56–57 (SorbyPhoto), 56rb (Scharfsinn), 58–59 (Denis Dymov), 58c (Macrovector), 59c & 96–97 (Parikh Mahendra N), 60–61 (Dmitry Chulov), 60br & 66lc (Orlok), 62–63 & 90–91 (Amors photos), 62bl (Jess Kraft), 63br (Federico Rostagno), 64–65 (Juice Flair), 64tr (Rejdan), 65tc (Marcin Balcerzak), 66–67 (Ajdin Kamber), 67tr (mikeledray), 68–69 (HappyTime19), 68br (Marianoblanco), 70–71 (Mazur Travel), 70rc (CRS PHOTO), 71br (KRISS75), 72–73 (Martyn Jandula), 72br (Pixel B), 73tl (Evgenii Panov), 74–75 (Volha Werasen), 74rc (BestPhotoPlus), 75tr (humphery), 76–77 (Morten B), 76rc (Prostock-studio), 77cl (Poravute Siriphiroon), 78br (Kekyalyaynen), 80–81 (studio23), 80br (PRESSLAB), 81tr (Anticiclo), 81cl (Crystal-K), 82–83 (Larina Marina), 82cr (Triawanda Tirta Aditya), 83tr (icosha), 84–85 (Aisyaqilumaranas), 84bl (Smile Fight), 86–87 (Yury Birukov), 86bl (ehasdemir), 88–89 (Andrey Armyagov), 89tr (Pierre-Yves Babelon), 90br (Dennis Wegewijs), 91br (Tatsiana Hendzel), 92–93 (clicksabhi), 94–95 (ivanbrunom), 94bl (RAMNIKLAL MODI), 95tl (Lucian Coman), 96–97 (Parikh Mahendra N), 96lc (kaetana), 97tr (PRILL), 98–99 (Belen B Massieu), 98bl (jennygiraffe), 99tr (Fabian Plock), 100bl (urfin), 101rc (Flystock), 102–103 (Avigator Fortuner), 102bc (Aleksey Petrakov), 104–105 (Make more Aerials), 104cr (Mr.B-king), 105cr (Frame Stock Footage), 106–107 (Photosebia), 106bl (Dipak Shelare), 108–109 (Canadapanda), 109tc (DashaR), 110–111 (Iryna Inshyna), 110bl (New Africa), 111rc (Billion Photos), 113t (ixpert), 114–115 (Panumas Yanuthai), 114rb (Yavuz Sariyildiz), 115tl (suprabhat), 116–117 (Frontpage), 116br (Patrick Poendl), 117tc (Oni Abimbola), 118–119 (Viktoriya Krayn), 118bl (Milosz Maslanka), 119cr (Jonathan Lingel), 120–121 (LUC BIANCO), 120cr (Yana Korn), 121tr (Evgeny_V), 122–123 (Nigel Jarvis), 122bl (kv naushad), 123tc (Goldilock Project), 124–125 (Syda Productions), 124cr (bakhistudio), 125cr (Candice Willmore).

This edition published in 2022 by Arcturus Publishing Limited
26/27 Bickels Yard, 151–153 Bermondsey Street,
London SE1 3HA

Copyright © Arcturus Holdings Limited

ISBN: 978-1-3988-2000-5
CH010347NT
Supplier 29, Date 0622, PI 00002252

Printed in China

Contributors: Helen Dwyer, James Nixon, Gill Humphrey, Alex Woolf, and Rachel Tilsdale
Consultant: Anne Rooney
Editors: Annabel Savery and Violet Peto
Designer: Lorraine Inglis
Picture research: Lorraine Inglis and Paul Futcher

CHILDREN'S ENCYCLOPEDIA OF THE ENVIRONMENT

CONTENTS

Introduction

Our environment is the world around us. Not just your bedroom, house, or street, but the wider world: the sky, land, rivers, oceans, deserts, and forests. The natural world gives us our weather, our food, and our health and well-being. But it is in trouble because human activity threatens ecosystems, habitats, and natural resources all over the world.

People and Animals

The population on Earth is growing. As it grows, there is increasing pressure to produce more and more food. However, we need to make sure the food we produce is healthy and that growing it does not damage the environment. As humans clear land for farming, fish the seas for food, and pollute waterways, it becomes harder for animals and plants to live. For some, life is so difficult that they are in danger of becoming extinct.

Changes in the climate make growing good crops more difficult.

Madame Berthe's mouse lemur is the smallest primate in the world and is critically endangered.

DID YOU KNOW? A change to our global temperature of just 1°C (2°F) causes more extreme weather events such as heatwaves, floods, and tornadoes.

Fossil Fuel Problems

Many homes, businesses, and countries depend on burning fossil fuels for energy and power. But the gases produced by burning fossil fuels are damaging the environment we rely on. The emissions from fossil fuels, along with other human activities, are causing our planet to warm up. Changes in the climate caused by global warming cause catastrophic problems—from flooding to habitat loss.

People still rely on energy from fossil fuels such as coal.

A World of People

As the human population grows, we are putting a huge strain on the natural environment. Resources, such as water, energy, wood, metals, and land, are becoming more stretched every day. Across the world, millions of people lack access to clean water, enough food, electricity, and modern technologies that might make their lives safer.

Many people in poorer countries do not have simple necessities, such as clean water and food.

Time to Clean Up

Humans create millions of tons of waste every day, causing countless problems for the environment. When harmful substances get into natural resources, they cause damage and make them dangerous to use. Gases can pollute the air, chemicals pollute waterways, and litter can pollute everywhere!

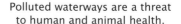

Polluted waterways are a threat to human and animal health.

Animals in Danger

Animals at risk of dying out are known as endangered species. Over the course of Earth's history, many species have become extinct. This means that there are no more of them living.

Rain Forest Species

Rain forests, thick with many types of plants, are a great habitat for a huge number of creatures. However, plants and animals that depend on the forest are now at risk because logging, farming, mining, and damming are destroying their precious habitats.

In the rain forests of Guinea in West Africa, open-pit mining is carried out to extract valuable minerals. Stripping away the soil exposes harmful chemicals. These are washed into the rivers, killing aquatic life.

All Earth's animals and plants depend on one another for their survival. Some animals eat plants as their food. They might become food for predators that eat other animals. The numbers of predators, prey, and plants are kept in balance by each other.

Rain forests are home to around 80% of the animals and plants that we have discovered, but they cover only 6% of the Earth's surface.

DESTROYING THE FOREST

In 2019, the area of rain forests destroyed in the tropics was the same as seven million football fields. Much forest is destroyed to make way for crops that will earn more money, such as palm oil.

DID YOU KNOW? Rain forests are finely balanced ecosystems. If a key species is lost, the whole system is threatened.

Communities of plants and animals that depend on each other are called ecosystems.

Some banana plants are grown in cleared areas of rain forest.

The Amazon river dolphin is threatened by mining and damming on the Amazon River in Brazil.

Beautiful Botos

Dolphins live in the Amazon River in South America. Their skin can be pink, and they are also known as "botos." Once thought of as magical creatures, they now come into conflict with humans who fish for catfish, the dolphin's prey. Hydroelectric dams built on the river and pollution released into it threaten the dolphin's habitat and food source.

African Wildlife

The continent of Africa is home to some of the world's most incredible wildlife. Many of the poorest countries on Earth are also in Africa.

Working with Wildlife

Africa accounts for 20% of Earth's land. It is home to thousands of animals and plants, many of which live only here. Poverty in many African countries puts a strain on resources, leading to reduced habitats and threats to wildlife. Many African animal species are now endangered.

Africa has many habitats, from jungles to deserts. Nature reserves and safari parks employ local people. If people can make a living from the wildlife, they are less likely to see it as a threat, as food, or as a resource to be sold.

Poachers target rhinos for their horns and elephants for their tusks. Trade in these items is banned, but criminals still sell them on the black market.

KEPT APART

Large areas of natural environments such as grasslands and forests have been split up by people building roads and cities. This prevents animals moving around freely to find food or mates. Shrinking habitats are a threat to their survival.

DID YOU KNOW? There are five species of rhino, some of which are nearly extinct. The White Rhino is the biggest species, weighing up to 3,500 kg (7,716 lb)!

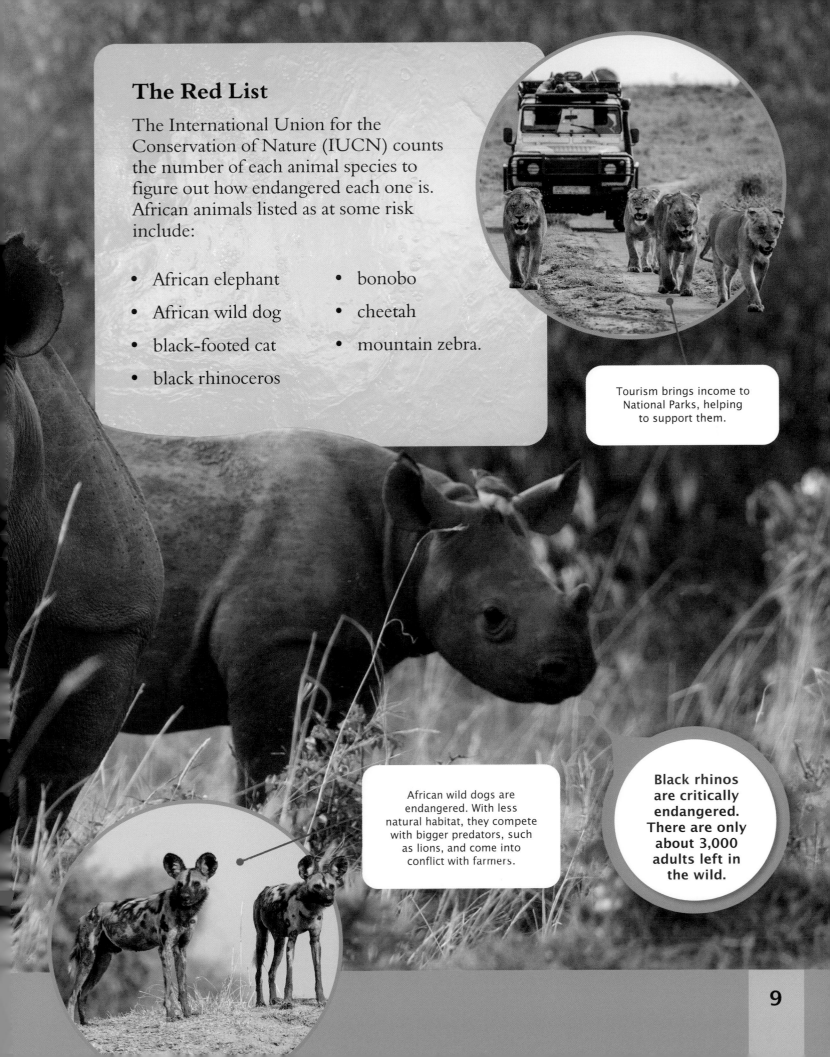

The Red List

The International Union for the Conservation of Nature (IUCN) counts the number of each animal species to figure out how endangered each one is. African animals listed as at some risk include:

- African elephant
- African wild dog
- black-footed cat
- black rhinoceros
- bonobo
- cheetah
- mountain zebra.

Tourism brings income to National Parks, helping to support them.

African wild dogs are endangered. With less natural habitat, they compete with bigger predators, such as lions, and come into conflict with farmers.

Black rhinos are critically endangered. There are only about 3,000 adults left in the wild.

Overfishing the Oceans

Oceans cover nearly three-quarters of the Earth. They contain thousands of species that depend on each other for survival.

Fishing the Seas

Overfishing means catching fish at a faster rate than stocks can naturally build up again. If too many young fish are caught, then populations cannot recover. Many countries have established limits on the number of fish that can be caught. Some have limited the size of nets to give young and smaller fish the chance to escape.

Overfishing is now the biggest threat to marine life.

Catching Tuna

The southern bluefin tuna is classified as endangered on the IUCN Red List. Tuna are targeted by fishing fleets because they fetch a high price at markets. Along with overfishing, bluefin tuna are threatened by disasters such as oil spills, which kill many young fish.

Tuna can dive deep and reach incredible speeds.

Fishing nets do not only trap the fish that fishers seek. Other fish including sharks and rays, and also dolphins, small whales, turtles, and seabirds, can all fall victim to nets.

Whales were hunted almost to extinction in the 1800s but are now protected.

IMPROVING PRACTICES

Many people around the world rely on fishing the oceans for food and income. Wildlife organizations are working together with fishing communities to improve sustainable fishing practices and protect marine ecosystems.

DID YOU KNOW? The number of large ocean fish today is just 10% of what it was before industrial fishing began in around the 1950s.

Species in Asia

The continent of Asia is home to more than half of the world's population. Its towns, cities, and farms are growing, threatening wildlife habitats.

Forest Guardians

Once found over a wide area from China to Java, today orangutans are found only in Borneo and Sumatra. Human activities such as logging and hunting have reduced their habitat, and their numbers have fallen to just half what they were a century ago. The Tapanuli orangutan is the most endangered of all ape species, with under 800 left in the wild.

As orangutans eat, they spread fruit seeds through the forest. This allows new plants to grow, keeping the forest healthy.

Habitat Loss

Asian elephants move from place to place in search of food and water. This often brings them into conflict with humans. Because of habitat loss, elephants sometimes eat grain crops on farmland, and many are killed each year. Around 40,000 to 50,000 Asian elephants remain in the wild.

Asian elephants have become endangered in the wild.

DID YOU KNOW? Orangutan means "forest person" in Malay.

Forest habitat is threatened as trees are cleared for agriculture. Orangutans are also hunted and their young kept as pets.

The slender loris is a tiny, monkey–like creature that lives in the forests of Sri Lanka. It is threatened by habitat loss and hunting. Traditional beliefs say that the slender loris has magical and medicinal powers, making them a target for poachers.

ASIAN ANIMALS IN DANGER

Pangolins, Sumatran tigers, clouded leopards, Javan rhinos, and lar gibbons are among the many other endangered Asian animals.

North American Wildlife

North America is home to many native species, including bison, bears, wolves, raccoons, rattlesnakes, and alligators. Over 2,000 animals and plants are listed as endangered or threatened in North America.

California Condor

The condor feeds on carrion (dead animals). They were driven to near extinction by the lead shot that hunters used on bigger animals because it poisoned the birds. By 1987, there were just 27 condors left in the wild. Condors were captured and placed in safe breeding facilities, then released back into the wild. Numbers have now risen to around 500 animals.

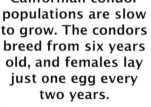

Californian condor populations are slow to grow. The condors breed from six years old, and females lay just one egg every two years.

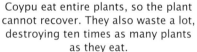

Coypu eat entire plants, so the plant cannot recover. They also waste a lot, destroying ten times as many plants as they eat.

Swamp Rat Takeover!

The coypu (also known as a swamp rat) is an invasive species introduced to the United States from South America in the 1930s. Since then, the coypu population has grown rapidly. They eat marsh plants, and their burrowing destroys the habitats of many native fish, crabs, and wetland birds. Invasive species often disrupt ecosystems.

INCREDIBLE CONDORS

An adult condor's wingspan can be 3 m (10 ft) from tip to tip. They glide on air currents, reaching heights of over 4,000 m (15,000 ft).

As human developments have increased, wild feeding lands of condors and other birds of prey have decreased.

Short-tailed albatrosses in Alaska are under threat. Fewer than 2,000 short-tailed albatrosses remain on Earth.

DID YOU KNOW? Short-tailed albatrosses are in danger from fishing lines, plastic and oil pollution, and from threats to their breeding sites.

Antarctic Wildlife

Antarctica is the world's most southerly continent. It is so cold, windy, and dry that few animals and plants can live there.

Warming Waters

Global warming is causing the Antarctic seas to warm up. This causes major changes to marine ecosystems. A rise of just 1°C (2°F) could allow new predators to move in. Sharks and king crabs living and hunting in the coastal waters could disrupt the food chains. The invaders would compete with native seabirds, seals, and whales for the fish and shellfish that live there.

A major threat to all Antarctic species is global warming. Rising temperatures reduce the amount of sea ice around the continent. This reduces penguin habitats and food supplies.

Fur seals were hunted to near extinction in the early 1900s but are now protected.

The First Link

Krill are tiny, shrimplike creatures that whales, seals, squid, and seabirds all depend on as a primary food source. Unfortunately, krill numbers are declining due to overfishing. Krill have also been losing their feeding grounds in the pack ice around the coast of Antarctica. The pack ice has been shrinking due to global warming.

Krill feed on phytoplankton, tiny plants that live in the water.

Emperor penguins can withstand temperatures of −50°C (−58°F). They have two layers of feathers, high body fat, and huddle together for warmth!

FUR SEALS

Most seals have a thick layer of fat under their skin called blubber, which keeps them warm. Fur seals also a have thick fur coat to keep them warm.

DID YOU KNOW? Antarctic krill are around the size of your little finger and can live in swarms big enough to be seen from space!

A Way Forward

Human activity has endangered and even wiped out many species on Earth. What can people do to reverse this trend?

Preserving Habitats

Animals cannot survive if their habitats are destroyed. We need global action to make sure the poorest people have space to farm and live without destroying the environments needed by the wildlife we share the planet with. Animals from elephants to insects and worms are threatened. We rely on the planet's biodiversity for our own survival.

Wildlife reserves can provide refuge for endangered species.

Ecotourism can help endangered species. Ecotourism encourages local people to earn a living from preserving endangered species.

We can play our part in helping to protect endangered species by supporting conservation projects and raising awareness.

DID YOU KNOW? Elephants can eat for up to 18 hours per day! Sadly, their constant need to find food can bring them into conflict with humans.

Pollution and climate change are two big threats to endangered animals. Anything we can do to reduce these will help, but large-scale actions by entire countries are difficult to bring about.

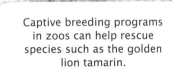

Captive breeding programs in zoos can help rescue species such as the golden lion tamarin.

Captive Breeding

In the early 1970s, there were only around 200 golden lion tamarins left in the wild. Conservationists began a captive breeding plan. Today, there are around 2,500 in the wild. But tamarins still face the problem of habitat loss, as their rain forest home is fragmented into small unconnected areas.

What Is Climate Change?

Climate change is a shift in the long-term weather and temperature patterns. It is a threat to life on our planet.

Heat from the Sun

The Sun gives out energy in the form of heat, light, and other forms of radiation. The Sun's heat warms Earth.

When the Sun's heat reaches Earth, some is reflected back into space and some is trapped by gases in the atmosphere. This is similar to how glass traps heat in a greenhouse, so it is known as the "greenhouse effect." The heat-trapping gases are called greenhouse gases. Greenhouse gases have built up over recent decades, causing global heating, which is changing the climate. The most important gases are carbon dioxide and methane.

Some heat reflected from Earth is trapped by the atmosphere.

A WARM WORLD

Our atmosphere and the greenhouse effect that it causes are essential to life on Earth. Without any greenhouse effect, the average temperature on Earth would be a chilly –18°C (0°F).

DID YOU KNOW? Scientists consider that Earth's atmosphere ends and space begins 100 km (62 mi) above Earth's surface.

The Sun gives us light and heat. Without it, life on Earth would not be possible.

The atmosphere is a layer of gases around Earth, a little bit like a blanket. It is made mostly of nitrogen and oxygen.

The carbon cycle shows the process of carbon moving through plants, animals, the ground, and into the air in carbon dioxide.

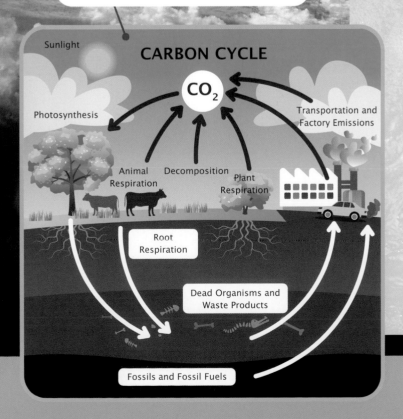

Sunlight

CARBON CYCLE

CO_2

Photosynthesis

Animal Respiration

Decomposition

Plant Respiration

Transportation and Factory Emissions

Root Respiration

Dead Organisms and Waste Products

Fossils and Fossil Fuels

Carbon Gases

Carbon dioxide is found naturally in the atmosphere. Plants take in carbon dioxide and use it to grow. Animals breathe it out as a waste gas. Carbon dioxide is also released when plants rot.

Humans have added carbon dioxide to the atmosphere by burning fossil fuels, such as coal, oil, and natural gas. Extracting fossil fuels releases methane into the air. Farming adds extra methane, too. These have contributed to global heating.

Causes of Climate Change

Climate change is happening because humans are adding more greenhouse gases to the atmosphere, especially carbon dioxide and methane.

How Is Carbon Dioxide Made?

Carbon is an element. It is all around us, all the time. It combines with other elements to form organic chemicals, and these are the basic building blocks for all life on Earth. Fossil fuels are formed from the remains of plants and animals that died millions of years ago. When they burn, the carbon in them combines with oxygen to create carbon dioxide.

We burn fossil fuels for energy. For example, we burn coal in power plants to generate electricity, and oil-based fuel in our cars.

Every time we go somewhere in a non-electric car, we add carbon dioxide to the atmosphere.

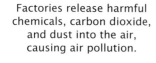

Factories release harmful chemicals, carbon dioxide, and dust into the air, causing air pollution.

NATURAL SOURCES

All humans and animals breathe out carbon dioxide, and it is released when plants decompose. It is also given out by volcanoes.

What Is Methane?

Methane is one of the greenhouse gases. Farm animals produce it when digesting food, and growing rice produces it. Mining coal and using natural gas produce it, and it is given out by landfill sites. By eating less meat and reducing fossil fuel use, we can cut methane emissions.

Methane from landfill sites can be captured and used to generate electricity.

The amount of carbon dioxide each of us produces is known as our carbon footprint. This includes the fuel we use and the fuel that is used to make and transport the things we buy.

DID YOU KNOW? People in wealthy countries have much larger carbon footprints than those in poorer countries.

Global Heating and Ice

Global heating is affecting the ice sheets at the North and South Poles. As the ice melts, sea levels will continue to rise.

Arctic Sea Ice

The central part of the Arctic Ocean is permanently frozen, forming a thick layer of sea ice. The ice sheet expands each winter and shrinks each summer. Over the last 40 years, scientists have been recording the extent of the sea ice. Their results show that sea ice is decreasing by 13% every ten years. Soon, there could be no summer sea ice at all.

The island of Greenland is covered by a sheet of ice and snow, but this ice cap is getting thinner.

Glaciers

Glaciers are slowly moving masses of ice that occur in the coldest places on Earth. When Glacier National Park, in the Rocky Mountains of the United States, was made into a national park in 1910, it had about 150 glaciers. Because of global warming, it now has just 25 named glaciers and they have all shrunk in recent decades.

The world's glaciers are shrinking due to global heating.

DID YOU KNOW? Glaciers can be thousands of years old. Scientists can study the air bubbles in them to find out about the past atmosphere.

A VICIOUS CYCLE

Bright–white snow and ice reflect the Sun's rays back into space. As ice melts, dark surfaces are revealed that absorb the Sun's heat. This causes temperatures to rise and more ice to melt.

The continent of Antarctica is covered with a thick sheet of ice and snow. This sheet holds around 70% of all the fresh water on Earth.

Melting ice on Greenland and in the Arctic will cause sea levels to rise. This will cause changes to ocean currents and weather patterns.

A Changing Climate

Global heating isn't only causing temperatures to rise, it's also causing other changes to the climate. These include a shift in rainfall patterns.

Oceans and Deserts

Rising temperatures disrupt the currents that move water around in the oceans, and these currents have impacts on weather. They affect the development of hurricanes, which form over the sea and move inland, and have an impact on both air temperature and rainfall.

Climate change has worsened natural weather patterns of floods and droughts. In dry areas, longer droughts threaten animals and plants. Bare soil is more easily worn away by wind and rain when it arrives, and nutrients in the soil will be lost. Farmers have to take over more natural land for farming as good soil is spoiled.

As the climate changes, patterns of rainfall will alter, with rain moving away from some areas. These areas will become drier and prone to droughts.

More extreme weather can cause forest fires, flooding, landslides, and drought. Cities, towns, and villages can be damaged by these events.

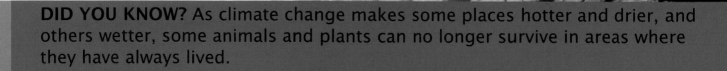

DID YOU KNOW? As climate change makes some places hotter and drier, and others wetter, some animals and plants can no longer survive in areas where they have always lived.

Global warming will cause some dry regions to become deserts.

Butterflies and Birds

In Europe, many types of butterfly have migrated north because temperatures in the south have become too warm. In North America, the breeding patterns of many species of migratory birds, such as the sooty shearwater, have also been affected.

Rising temperatures and changing weather patterns are affecting plants and animals.

CHANGING TOO FAST

Changes in climate happen naturally on Earth over time, but the speed of recent changes is the result of human activity.

Extreme Weather

Extreme weather is becoming more frequent as the climate changes, threatening humans and other species.

Flooding

There have been many disastrous floods in different parts of the world in recent years. These are due to unusually heavy rains, hurricanes, and storms. They also result from changes in land use and increases in the size of urban areas. A rise in sea levels has made coastal flooding more likely. In 2020, record rainfall caused floods in Indonesia, Kenya, Uganda, Bangladesh, China, Sudan, Nigeria, and Nicaragua.

This satellite image shows Hurricane Katrina moving toward the US coast in 2005.

A storm triggered severe flooding in Thailand during the 2011 monsoon season.

Storm Season

The year 2005 broke all records for storms in the western Atlantic. There were 28 severe storms, 15 hurricanes, and seven major hurricanes. Three, including Hurricane Katrina, reached wind speeds of over 251 kph (156 mph). In the same year, three big cyclones hit Australia.

Floodwaters bring many dangers. As well as destroying homes, they can carry dangerous debris and damage food supplies. Their dirty water can spread disease.

28

Long dry seasons, high temperatures, lightning, and strong winds all cause wildfires. In 2020, California, Greece, Turkey, Siberia, and the Amazon rain forest experienced devastating wildfires.

JL. YOS SUDARSO 3
BLOK J.1, J.2

IGNORING EVIDENCE

Some people still do not believe that human activity has led to the changes in our climate and extreme weather events. Climate scientists all agree that humans are responsible, and point to ways of slowing heating.

DID YOU KNOW? A heatwave is a period when summer temperatures are well above normal. Heatwaves have become more common in recent years.

Food, Water, and Disease

Water supplies can become so low in some places that people must walk long distances to collect it.

Global warming is likely to affect the world's supply of food and water, and cause certain diseases to spread.

Enough Water

Safe drinking water is a precious resource in dry parts of the world, such as North Africa. A rise in sea levels may cause salt water to enter groundwater and contaminate some freshwater supplies. At the same time, dry areas are expected to become drier.

Higher temperatures and drought are likely to affect farmers in the warmer parts of the world. In the tropics, where lots of the world's food is grown, some crops may become impossible to grow because it is too hot and dry.

It is difficult for farmers to grow crops in dry soil.

YOUNG AND OLD

Everyone is likely to be affected by climate change, but the elderly and the very young will be most at risk from heat-related illnesses, especially if they are poor or do not have access to enough food.

DID YOU KNOW? Hotter weather and more rain could increase numbers of insects called ticks, which spread Lyme disease to humans.

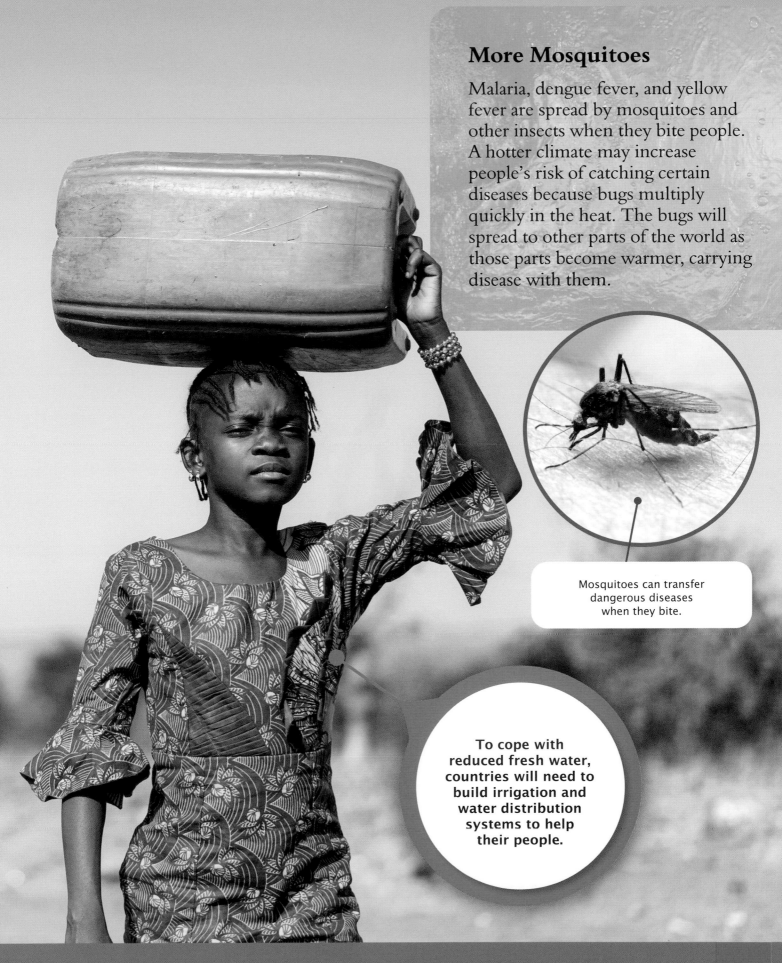

More Mosquitoes

Malaria, dengue fever, and yellow fever are spread by mosquitoes and other insects when they bite people. A hotter climate may increase people's risk of catching certain diseases because bugs multiply quickly in the heat. The bugs will spread to other parts of the world as those parts become warmer, carrying disease with them.

Mosquitoes can transfer dangerous diseases when they bite.

To cope with reduced fresh water, countries will need to build irrigation and water distribution systems to help their people.

A Green Future

We need to slow, stop, and then reverse global warming. This means reducing carbon dioxide emissions as fast as possible.

Clean Energy

There are many energy sources that do not release greenhouse gases. These include wind power, solar power, and wave power. These may not be able to fuel our cars directly, but they can generate electricity, and we can use that to power transportation. Already, many countries are turning to these "clean" energy sources to provide at least some of their energy.

Although green energy forms are not entirely carbon-free, they produce less emissions than fossil fuels.

Although electric vehicles do not produce emissions when they run, emissions are given out when they and their batteries are made.

Working Together

Global warming is an international issue, and governments must act together to reduce carbon emissions. They do this by trying to reach agreement at climate conferences on how much each country is allowed to emit. Emissions targets were agreed for wealthy countries at COP26 (the United Nations Climate Change Conference) in 2021.

DID YOU KNOW? Choosing to travel on foot or by bike can help your health, as well as the health of the planet!

Norway produces around 45% of its energy from hydropower. Electricity is produced as water flows through turbines in huge dams. Brazil and New Zealand are big renewable energy producers.

DOING OUR PART

Everyone can help reduce greenhouse gas emissions. We can save fuel by using public transportation and by walking or cycling instead of driving whenever possible. We can eat less meat and fewer dairy products, and take fewer or no flights.

Food and Farming

We all need food, and we get most of our food from farming. Farmers rely on the environment to produce our food, yet many farming practices harm it.

Food and the Environment

Producing our food has an impact on the environment in many ways. The methods used to farm animals and crops, the moving of produce around the world, and even the locations we choose to grow particular crops can cause environmental damage if we make the wrong choices. Poor choices can also harm the people involved in farming.

Foods that keep well and are not delicate can be moved around with little wastage. If food spoils, the resources used to grow it have been wasted.

While a lot of food is grown in developing countries, often it is exported away from local populations.

Far and Wide

People in developed countries have a wide choice of food. Some of it is grown far away, often in developing countries. Crops often grow well in hot countries, but they take a lot of water and land, using resources local people need to grow food to eat themselves.

Food that is produced far from where it is eaten has to be transported long distances. Some is wasted because it spoils before arrival.

DID YOU KNOW? We all depend on a diet of nutritious food for a healthy life!

Fruit and vegetables are good for you, but not always for the environment—it depends on how they are grown.

Food collects "food miles" as it travels. This is a measure of how far it has moved. High mileage often means that more environmental harm has been caused in bringing it to you.

CROSSING BORDERS

Food is produced and transported all over the world, which causes environmental damage. It's better to choose food moved by ship rather than by plane if possible, as ships cause less harm than planes.

Animals and Our Food

People around the world are eating more meat, eggs, and milk. All this comes from animals. How we farm animals affects the environment.

It is important for animals to have a good standard of living and a healthy diet, not only for their own benefit but to protect the environment.

Keeping Animals

Farm animals are healthiest when they have enough space, fresh air, and suitable food. Pressure on farmers to produce more and more food has led to many keeping animals in overcrowded conditions. Their waste pollutes the soil, air, and water, and the animals themselves suffer.

Even fish can be farmed. Fish farming can damage the environment if not carried out responsibly. The food fed to farmed fish is often made from wild-caught fish or crops such as soybeans, farmed in areas where rain forest has been removed.

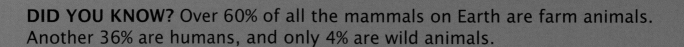

36   **DID YOU KNOW?** Over 60% of all the mammals on Earth are farm animals. Another 36% are humans, and only 4% are wild animals.

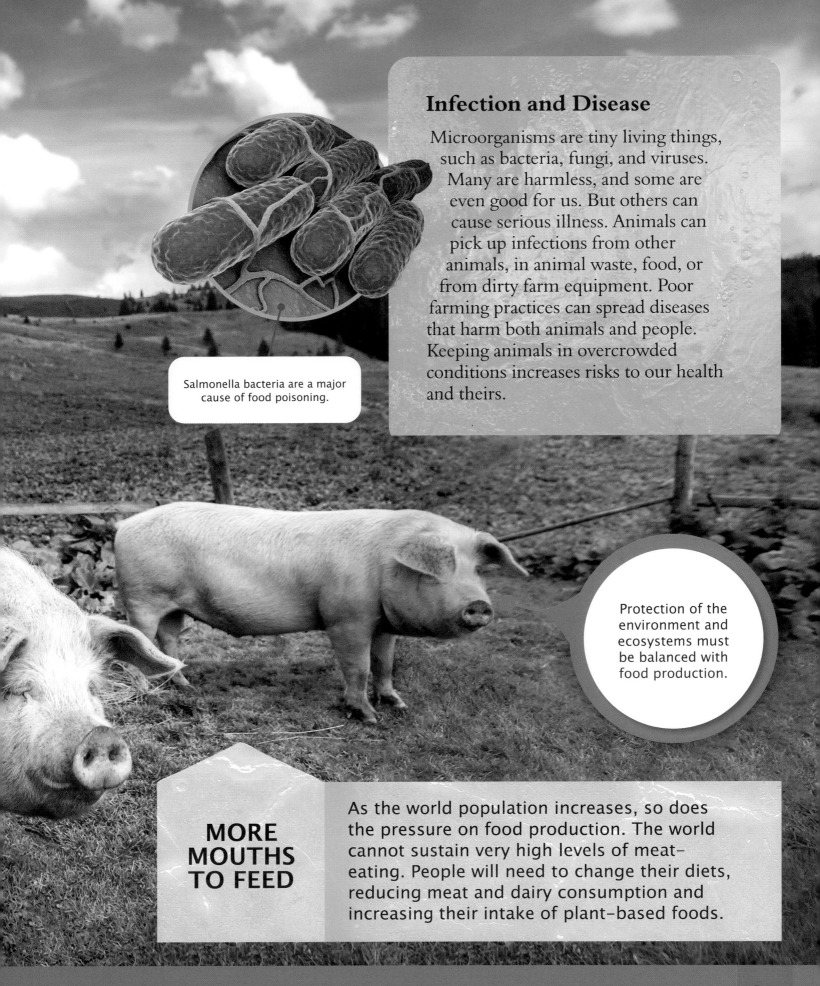

Infection and Disease

Microorganisms are tiny living things, such as bacteria, fungi, and viruses. Many are harmless, and some are even good for us. But others can cause serious illness. Animals can pick up infections from other animals, in animal waste, food, or from dirty farm equipment. Poor farming practices can spread diseases that harm both animals and people. Keeping animals in overcrowded conditions increases risks to our health and theirs.

Salmonella bacteria are a major cause of food poisoning.

Protection of the environment and ecosystems must be balanced with food production.

MORE MOUTHS TO FEED

As the world population increases, so does the pressure on food production. The world cannot sustain very high levels of meat-eating. People will need to change their diets, reducing meat and dairy consumption and increasing their intake of plant-based foods.

Plants and Our Food

Farmers often grow huge fields of one type of plant, cutting down hedgerows and woodland. To produce a strong, healthy crop, many farmers use chemicals to prevent disease, get rid of weeds and pests, and increase the amount of food produced.

Using Chemicals

Farmers use herbicides on their crops to kill weeds. Pesticides are used to prevent insects, slugs, and other creatures from eating the crop. Some of these pesticides remain on the plant's surface and kill the pest when they make contact with it. Other pesticides are taken up by the plant and kill the pest when they eat it. When birds and other animals eat pests that have taken in pesticides, they can be poisoned.

Chemicals sprayed on plants can sometimes damage natural ecosystems.

Chemicals sprayed on plants are tightly managed by governments. Farmers have to be careful how much and where they use them.

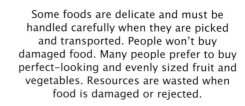

Some foods are delicate and must be handled carefully when they are picked and transported. People won't buy damaged food. Many people prefer to buy perfect-looking and evenly sized fruit and vegetables. Resources are wasted when food is damaged or rejected.

ORGANIC FARMING

Some farms produce food without using chemical pesticides, herbicides, or fertilizer. These are known as organic farms. Organic farming is better for the environment, but it is more costly for farmers.

Farmers use big machines to spread fertilizer over crops.

Using Fertilizer

To get the best possible yield from their crop, farmers need the plants to grow big and strong.

Some farmers spray the crops with fertilizers, which contain added nutrients that help the plants grow. However, these fertilizers can be washed from the soil into rivers and lakes. This can harm fish that live in the water and also animals that graze on the land.

DID YOU KNOW? Around 60% of the calories we take in from plants comes from three key crops: rice, corn, and wheat!

Food Miles

Long ago, people could only eat food grown in their local area or their own country. Now, refrigerated trucks, planes, and ships mean that we can eat food from around the world. But this has an impact on the environment.

Planes, Ships, Trains, and Trucks

Moving food around the world uses a great deal of fossil fuels to power the planes, ships, trains, and trucks used. Using fossil fuels adds carbon emissions and pollution to the air. Carbon emissions are a major source of global heating, which is damaging the climate and environment.

It's usually best to buy food that has been locally produced if possible. But it's not entirely simple. A food that has been moved a long distance by ship might still be better for the environment than one which has been a flown a shorter distance, since air transportation produces more emissions than shipping. Some foods need other resources, such as fuel for heating, if they are grown locally. It's a complex calculation.

Cocoa beans used for chocolate are grown in South America. They can be transported by ship, so even moving them a long way is not too harmful.

WATER SUPPLIES

Foods such as oranges and almonds take a lot of water to grow. Often, they are grown in hot regions where water is already scarce. Using up the water supply damages the environment and threatens people who live in the area.

Read the Label

Some products, such as soybean oil, can be produced in a sustainable, responsible way, or grown in an environmentally damaging way, such as in areas of cleared rain forest. The packaging often tells you if a product has been produced sustainably.

Some food manufacturers label products with information telling you where they have come from and how they were produced.

Bread is often produced locally, but the flour used to make it might have come from a long way away.

DID YOU KNOW? A study of a Christmas meal eaten in Britain found that the food miles of the ingredients added up to ten trips around the world.

41

Food Chains

Food chains show how living things depend on each other, with each one feeding on another in the chain. Food chains show the transfer of energy (from food) between organisms, starting with plants.

Our Place in the Food Chain

All food chains start with plants, which make food using the energy of the sun and chemicals from the soil and air. They provide food for plant-eating animals (herbivores). In turn, these are eaten by meat-eaters (carnivores). It takes many herbivores to support a carnivore.

Energy is lost moving through a food chain, as each animal uses some of the energy it takes in to move and run its body. Not all its food is turned into meat! For this reason, farming plants produces more food energy from the same amount of land as raising animals for meat.

Plants are at the base of every food chain. They produce seeds and leaves that are eaten by herbivores and omnivores.

MARINE FOOD CHAINS

Many food chains in water habitats begin with phytoplankton. These tiny organisms make food using sunlight and are eaten by bigger creatures.

DID YOU KNOW? Food chains can even form deep under the ocean, where minerals escape through Earth's crust through cracks called vents and nourish microbes!

Industrial processes can release harmful chemicals into the air.

Air Pollution

If chemicals are used in farming and land management, or are present in the air, soil, or water through pollution, they can enter the food chain.

Small birds and insects take in low levels of chemical pollutants when they feed on plants. Predators that eat the birds and insects then take in the chemical, too, and end up with a larger amount in their bodies. Predators at the top of the food chain may end up with dangerously high levels of chemicals in their bodies. Even humans can take in poisons from food in this way.

Growing only one type of plant in an area can harm the environment and disrupt food chains. A healthy environment has many different kinds of organisms

When animals die, their bodies decompose, adding nutrients to the soil. Plants then use the nutrients to grow. This is called the nutrient cycle.

Avoiding Food Waste

Wasting food is a huge problem for the environment and for people. Reducing waste can help food security and the environment.

Food can be preserved by salting, pickling, or drying. These are ancient methods used before modern science.

Take Care

Food is wasted during production and transportation, but also in stores and people's homes. Resources such as land, water, fertilizers, fuel for farm vehicles, and transportation have all been invested in food, all at a cost to the environment. We need to avoid waste whenever possible.

At home, people can buy and cook only what they need, and use any leftovers. There are many ways to prevent food going bad, to avoid waste.

Dairy foods are often pasteurized to make them last longer.

ADDING CHEMICALS

Preservatives are chemicals that can be added to food to prevent bacteria from growing, so that food lasts longer. Some foods work naturally as preservatives. Sugar, salt, and vinegar all help to protect food from spoiling.

DID YOU KNOW? Astronauts living on the International Space Station eat food that is dried and vacuum-packed to make it last a long time!

Soft fruits such as strawberries and raspberries are often preserved using a form of radiation that kills microorganisms.

Vacuum-packing foods prevents air from getting to them. This means that bacteria cannot grow.

Other Ways of Keeping Food Fresh

Foods can be vacuum-packed. This involves sucking the air out of the packaging around the food to make it last longer.

Modified atmosphere packaging is used to keep salad leaves fresh for longer. This technique involves changing the atmosphere inside the food packaging, so that it contains less oxygen and more carbon dioxide. The carbon dioxide kills bacteria, and therefore the salad leaves last longer.

45

What Are Fossil Fuels?

Fuels are materials that we burn to make heat or power. Fossil fuels formed millions of years ago from the remains of plants and animals. We use three types of fossil fuels: coal, oil, and natural gas.

How Fossil Fuels Formed

In prehistoric times, when plants and animals died, they sank into the ground. Layers of sand, mud, and clay built up above their remains. After millions of years, the pressure and heat below these layers chemically changed the animal and plant remains, changing them into coal, oil, and natural gas.

Today, around 84% of all the energy used in the world comes from fossil fuels. We use fossil fuels for most of our everyday energy needs. They have a terrible impact on the environment. We need to move to different sources of energy.

Most coal was formed long ago when much of Earth was covered with swamps and forests.

We use fossil fuels to heat our homes, cook our food, and power our cars.

DID YOU KNOW? Scientists predict that coal reserves will last over 100 years, and oil and gas reserves around 50 years.

Uses and Problems

Fossil fuels are not used only for energy. Crude oil can be refined into many products including chemicals used to make plastics and paints. Fossil fuels can damage the environment in whichever way they are used. Coal-fired power plants pollute the air. Waste from oil refineries contaminates local water sources. Plastics remain in the environment for hundreds of years.

Oil is transported across the sea in ships called tankers. The biggest can carry 3.7 million barrels of oil!

Human dependence on fossil fuels is causing huge problems for the natural world.

GLOBAL WARMING

Burning fossil fuels produces gases such as carbon dioxide. These gases trap the Sun's heat inside Earth's atmosphere, causing temperatures on Earth to increase. This is called global warming.

Finding and Using Coal

Coal is a black or brown rocky material. It is widely used as a fuel and is often burned to generate electricity.

Wood from the Past

Coal has formed over millions of years from trees and other plants that lived in the distant past. When they died, instead of being broken down and their chemicals recycled, they were turned first into peat and eventually into coal by heat and pressure underground. Most of the coal we use now has come from trees growing 300-350 million years ago.

When the trees were living, they took carbon dioxide out of the air and locked the carbon away in their trunks and branches. When we burn that coal now, we release the carbon dioxide into our atmosphere. It builds up, heating the world.

Coal miners work deep underground, using drills and other machines to cut the coal from the surrounding rock.

Anthracite is a very hard, shiny, black form of coal.

USING MORE COAL

For thousands of years, coal has been used as a source of heat. In the eighteenth century, it also began to be used as fuel to power machines in factories. In the nineteenth century, coal started to be used to generate electricity.

Coal Mining

Coal can be found both close to the surface and deeper underground. Surface mining scrapes back the landscape to dig out the valuable coal. In underground mining, shafts are dug deep into the ground to extract the coal. Surface mines damage wildlife habitats and cause problems such as landslides and floods. The waste from coal mines is toxic and can pollute nearby ecosystems.

The upper levels of natural environment are removed to expose layers of coal below.

Some coal deposits are covered by only a few thin layers of rock and soil.

Using Oil and Natural Gas

Oil is a thick, dark liquid. Natural gas is found above it, trapped underground.

Oil and Gas

Natural gas and oil deposits are often found together. At gas-oil separation plants, the two fuels are separated.

In 1859, people began drilling for oil and pumping it to the surface. Oil that comes out of the ground is called crude oil. It is sent through pipelines to refineries, where it is turned into more useful products. Millions of barrels of oil make their way from producers to consumers every day.

A lot of oil and gas deposits are under the ocean. Large floating platforms are built to hold the drilling equipment needed to bring the oil and gas to the surface.

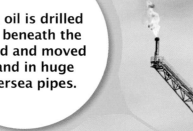

Much oil is drilled from beneath the seabed and moved to land in huge undersea pipes.

Plastic is easy to produce— but very hard to get rid of.

Plastic Products

Besides being used as a fuel, oil is used to make plastic products, such as bottles, asphalt (used to pave roads), waterproofing materials, and fabrics such as nylon and acrylic. Plastic does not break down chemically in the environment, so plastic waste is an increasing problem.

DID YOU KNOW? Tiny bits of plastic (called microplastics) are now found everywhere, even inside human bodies.

OIL SPILLS

Sometimes, accidents occur during the drilling or transportation of crude oil, and it spills into the ocean. Oil can spill from tankers, offshore platforms, or from oil wells.

Oil spills contaminate coastlines and can kill hundreds of thousands of fish, seabirds, and other animals.

As reserves decline, people are looking for new places to drill for oil. As more oil drilling takes place, more natural habitats are disturbed, damaged, and destroyed.

End of Oil?

As the world's population expands, demand for energy is increasing. New solutions need to be found for both people and our planet.

Looking Beyond Oil

In response to the growing need for energy and its high costs, some oil companies are trying a new method of recovering more oil called "fracking." This fractures rock underground using a high-pressure mix of water, sand, and chemicals to release its gas.

Fracking is damaging to the environment, and the fossil fuel recovered will do further harm when used. It has been linked with small earthquakes in some areas, and many people oppose it. To protect the environment, we need to look beyond fossil fuels.

The Trans-Alaska Pipeline has carried oil across Alaska since 1977. It now operates at only a fraction of its full capacity.

The Arctic fox is part of the ecosystem of the northern polar region.

RENEWABLE ENERGY

Wind, solar, geothermal, and hydro are forms of renewable energy that are all alternatives to using fossil fuels. Fossil fuels will still be used, but their use must decrease.

The Trans-Alaska Pipeline carries crude oil 1,200 km (756 mi) across the state of Alaska, USA.

Nuclear Power

Nuclear power harnesses the energy unleashed by the splitting of an atom. It is a possible alternative to fossil fuels. Nuclear power plants produce energy without producing greenhouse gases. However, nuclear power produces radioactive waste, which is difficult to dispose of. It will remain dangerous for hundreds or thousands of years. The risk of accidents at nuclear power plants worries many people.

A vast area around the Chernobyl nuclear power plant was evacuated after a disaster there in 1986.

DID YOU KNOW? China's East–West gas pipeline extends for over 8,700 km (5.406 mi).

A Global Market

Fossil fuel deposits are scattered unevenly around the planet. Some countries are dependent on others to supply their energy needs.

Working Across Borders

Since countries have different fuel resources, oil and gas are supplied by one country to another. When there is a conflict between nations or a disagreement about prices, supplies can be stopped. This causes problems in countries that do not have their own fuel reserves. For example, fuel prices can become very high, and people struggle to pay energy bills.

A move to renewable sources of energy would give more countries control over their own energy supply. Oil-producing nations and organizations are fighting to keep oil flowing because they depend on money from oil. Some have argued that climate change is not caused by the use of fossil fuels, but others are now beginning to invest in renewable energy sources.

Oil provides the main source of income for many countries in the Middle East, including Saudi Arabia.

LEAVING OIL IN THE GROUND

If alternative energy supplies can be developed, we can stop taking coal, oil, and gas from the ground to burn. Ancient carbon can then remain locked away where it has been for millions of years, harmlessly.

DID YOU KNOW? Many countries are now promising to reduce their use of coal-fired power plants to try and slow global warming.

Much of the oil supply in the Middle East comes from an area called the Arabian–Iranian Sedimentary Basin.

Price Protests

In 2022, fuel costs rose dramatically around the world, causing protests and hardship for people. While oil-producing nations tried to increase production, other countries realized they needed to rely more on energy from renewable sources.

Gas extracted in Kazakhstan is mostly sold outside the country.

The Way Forward

There are many things we can do to reduce our use of fossil fuels and use more renewable energy sources.

Help from Governments

Using less fossil fuel depends both on individual choices and on government policy and investment. Governments must invest in green energy solutions, such as renewable energy plants and electric cars, and move away from fossil fuel sources. Homes must be built to be energy-efficient, so that less energy is used keeping them warm. Better public transportation would allow individuals to use cars less. The use of plastic packaging can be regulated by laws.

Wind turbines are one way to generate clean energy. Wind's movement energy is turned into electrical energy using generators.

Light Emitting Diode (LED) light bulbs use far less energy than traditional ones.

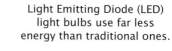

DID YOU KNOW? The world's wealthiest nations are the biggest producers of dangerous greenhouse gases.

Changing Our Ways

There are many things that we can do in our daily lives to reduce the amount of power we use. These include:

- turning off appliances when we aren't using them
- turning down the heating in winter and wearing a sweater
- walking, riding a bike, or using public transportation instead of using the car, and
- swapping the family car for an electric one, or none at all.

If we recycle paper, cans, and plastic products, less energy is used making new products.

Solar panels change the Sun's heat energy into electrical energy. A big field of solar panels is called a solar farm.

WITHOUT POWER

While many think of access to electricity and fuel as "normal," there are millions of people around the world who do not have access to either.

A Growing Population

The number of people on the planet today puts huge stress on resources. With more people, we use more land, fuel, water, and other resources.

More People

Throughout most of history, the human population has grown slowly. However, in the last 100 years, there has been enormous growth.

The biggest cities have over 37 million people living in them. All of these people need food, water, and housing.

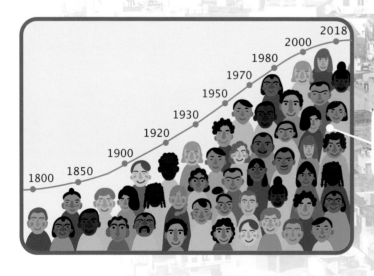

This graph shows the sharp increase in the world's population, particularly since 1800.

The highest rate of growth happened in the late 1960s. By 1999, the human population had doubled from 3 billion to 6 billion in just 36 years. Today, the world population increases by around 82 million people each year. Country populations are affected not only by births and deaths, but also by people migrating between countries.

DID YOU KNOW? Since the beginning of human history, most humans have lived in Asia.

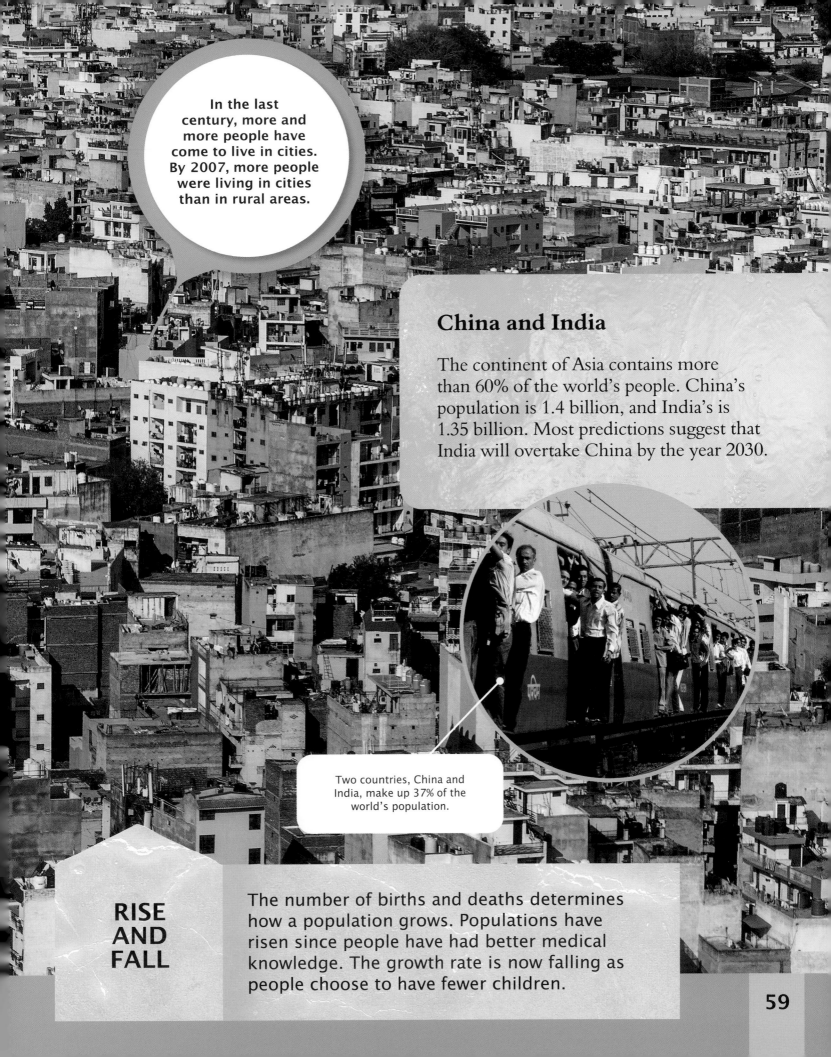

In the last century, more and more people have come to live in cities. By 2007, more people were living in cities than in rural areas.

China and India

The continent of Asia contains more than 60% of the world's people. China's population is 1.4 billion, and India's is 1.35 billion. Most predictions suggest that India will overtake China by the year 2030.

Two countries, China and India, make up 37% of the world's population.

RISE AND FALL

The number of births and deaths determines how a population grows. Populations have risen since people have had better medical knowledge. The growth rate is now falling as people choose to have fewer children.

Areas in Crisis

The population is growing much more quickly in developing regions of the world, such as countries in Southeast Asia. This puts stress on resources and the environment in areas where they are already stretched.

Population Pressure

Bangladesh is a very poor country and has one of the highest population densities in the world. The overcrowding is so great that it reduces the quality of life, damages the environment, and leads to a shortage of services and goods.

Nigeria is the most populated country in Africa with over 211 million people. Nigeria has one of the highest birth rates in the world. The population is set to rise to 400 million by 2050. How will the country cope? Health care and living conditions are poor in many parts of Nigeria. Only 68% of the population has access to clean water.

Rickshaws create traffic jams in the streets of Dhaka in Bangladesh. This method of transportation is climate-friendly.

Falling Populations

The population is not growing in every part in the world. In some countries, many people are leaving to look for a better life. In other countries, it is falling because of war, famine, or disease. In some countries, people are having fewer children.

War and fighting in Syria have caused people to leave in search of a safer place to live.

DID YOU KNOW? Population density measures how crowded a country or city is.

Bangladesh has one of the highest population densities, with an average of over 400 people per square km (0.4 square mi). In comparison, Canada has an average of just 4 people per square km (0.4 square mi).

HOW MANY PEOPLE LIVE HERE?

The United States has the third–largest population in the world but a population density of only 30 people per square km (0.4 square mi). Some developed countries, such as Britain and the Netherlands, have a dense population, putting strain on some resources.

Using up Resources

In 1798, mathematician Thomas Malthus concluded that the number of humans would one day outgrow the food supply. This would result in mass starvation.

Facing Hard Times

Food is not the only resource that people need, and others are in danger of running out soon. Climate change and changes to the land puts pressure on resources that grow, like wood and cotton. Metals that we use for all kinds of electronic equipment are mined, reducing supplies underground.

A lot of the things we take for granted in our daily lives will become more expensive as the resources needed to make them become scarce and go up in price. People in countries that have become rich recently, such as China, want the consumer goods already common in richer countries, so demand will increase further.

Statues on Rapa Nui were created by ancient peoples living there from 300 CE.

Island Life

Rapa Nui, a tiny island in the Pacific Ocean, was densely populated in 1650. By the end of the nineteenth century, the island was bare, and the population was just over 100. Trees had been cut down, leading to a loss of wood for fuel and boatbuilding. Without boats, the people could not fish for food.

NATURAL RESOURCES

Natural resources are anything that a country has from nature and which it can use. This might include fossil fuels, minerals, forests, farmland, or access to bodies of water.

Water shortages are a problem around the world. Water is used for industry, as well as for growing food.

Rich countries, particularly in Europe and North America, continue to use up resources at a fast rate.

DID YOU KNOW? People are living beyond what the planet can provide for us. People in rich countries use more than their fair share of resources.

Land Under Pressure

A growing population puts pressure on land, not just to live on, but also to produce food. Today, more than 34% of the world's land is being used to grow crops or raise livestock.

Changing the Land

Every plot of land taken for farming reduces the space available for wildlife and for trees to restore oxygen to the air. Already, our ecosystem is threatened by the changes we have made to the land, cutting down forests and clearing vast areas for farming.

The soil is changed by farming single crops or keeping farm animals intensively. It is not as rich, or home to as many organisms, as the soils in forest, woodland, or natural grassland. Clearing land of trees over a large area even changes local weather patterns. As the population increases, we need better land management.

Land that is overused often stops being able to produce crops.

GROWING FOOD

Of the world's land, 27% is used to raise animals and 7% is used to grow crops. It is more efficient to raise and eat plants than animals.

People disagree as to whether plants' genes should be altered.

Can Science Help?

Science can help to tackle the pressure on land in several ways. Genetic engineering can modify plants so that they can grow in salty or dry soils. "Vertical farming" involves growing crops in towers or up the sides of walls and buildings. Meat grown in a factory from cells is an alternative to farming animals.

To keep pace with a growing population, countries started to produce crops on a large scale.

Growing one type of crop plant in an area is called monoculture. It can lead to problems with low biodiversity.

DID YOU KNOW? It takes about 100 years for natural processes to make 2.5 cm (1 in) of new topsoil.

65

Driven Out

People who live in poverty or dangerous places often try to migrate to another country. As climate change increases, more people will need to migrate.

Seeking Survival

A lack of food, water, and shelter can lead to migration even now. People already leave their homes because of wars and natural disasters. As some areas become too hot and dry to live in and farm, or are flooded by rising sea levels, many more people will move around looking for somewhere safe to live.

Large numbers of people moving into an area quickly put pressure on resources. It can cause conflict because people resist newcomers, especially if their supplies of food and water are already under strain. Wars will become more common as people fight for resources.

People leave countries to escape from war, poverty, hunger, or natural disasters. Countries that take in migrants must provide for them.

People migrate to find safer places to live, but they often meet with more conflict. This problem will become worse.

REFUGEE CRISIS

When people's lives are in danger, they go and look for safety and refuge in a different place. They are called refugees. Sometimes, there are so many refugees that other countries cannot take them all in, and a crisis forms. Climate change will bring more refugees.

More Migrants

As climate change causes sea levels to rise, coastal areas, including many cities, will flood and become uninhabitable. Large numbers of people will have to move out. Where will these millions of people move to? There is no easy answer to this question.

Migrants and refugees will settle in a new area for a while. But for how long will it be safe?

When the land can no longer support its inhabitants, people will have to move.

DID YOU KNOW? In 2020, there were 281 million international migrants. By 2050, experts predict there will be more than a billion climate refugees.

67

Older Populations

In an older population, there is more pressure on health and welfare services.

In the early 1800s, life expectancy globally was around 40 years. Today, it is 70 years. This means that the populations of many countries are getting older.

Living Longer

Advances in technology and improved health care causes death rates to fall, especially in the developed world. Researchers think that one in every six people will be over the age of 60 by the year 2030.

Retired people do not work and pay less taxes. Younger people work more and pay more taxes to governments. Less money coming into governments means that it is harder for them to support the growing number of older people, who are likely to have health care needs.

Countries in sub–Saharan Africa such as Niger and Mali have a high birth rate and a young dependent population.

Dependent Population

The very young and the very old are known as dependents, since they depend on working-age people for support. In some countries, there are more young dependent people of 0 to 14 years than older people. With a very young population, it is hard for governments to provide education and heath care for everyone.

DID YOU KNOW? Singapore has a rapidly aging population—the life expectancy is 83 years.

Japan has an older population. The Japanese government have put money into technologies and care systems that support elderly people.

ALL FAIR

Young people will grow up to be workers and pay taxes; older people have previously worked and paid taxes. We are all dependents for part of our lives, and society must be structured to support older and younger people.

More People

As the population increases, it will put more strain on natural resources and the environment. It is important that we find ways of sharing fairly.

Managing Resources

Many experts believe that if Earth's natural resources were managed better, they could support the present population and more. Future technologies may help to increase the supply of food and energy resources without damaging the environment too much.

Improving quality of life is the best way to tackle overpopulation. When people are better educated and have a higher standard of living, they have fewer children. This is the fairest way to limit population growth.

While some have plenty to eat, others have little. Some regions are more fertile than others, leading to a higher abundance of food.

India's government needs to support large numbers of young children.

POLLUTION PROBLEMS

With a higher world population, there will be higher levels of pollution unless waste is managed well. Water is polluted by sewage and chemicals, land by litter, and air by gases produced by industry and vehicle emissions.

Even if a region produces a lot of food, good food does not reach everyone who needs it. Much might be sold abroad or into richer areas where it fetches a higher price.

Future Planning

Resources such as forests and farmland must not be overused to the point of destruction. Richer countries must help poorer nations to save resources by using renewable energy and recycling. If infrastructure, transportation, schools, and housing are improved, countries will be able to cope with rising populations.

Developing nations need investment in new technologies to help them grow without harming the environment.

DID YOU KNOW? Each extra person born into a wealthy country will use more resources than a person born into poor country.

A Polluted Planet

Pollution happens when dangerous substances get into our environment. Pollution can damage the plants and animals that live around us and harm our health.

Fossil Fuels

Coal, oil, and gas are fossil fuels. They were formed underground millions of years ago. Burning these fuels to create energy releases poisonous substances and gases. These get into the air we breathe, the water we drink, and the soil we grow our food on.

Most cars burn fossil fuels and so do many power plants. That is why everyday activities, such as driving to school or using electricity, create pollution. The most polluted places in the world are large, crowded cities.

Burning coal in power plants causes both air and water pollution. This causes health problems for us and our planet.

Pollution All Around

The quality of air in cities is constantly measured and reported. But pollution also affects soil and water. These are monitored in many places because they affect people. Other types of pollution affect wildlife more than humans. Noise and light pollution disturb the habits and life cycles of many organisms.

Buildings, cars, industry, and traffic all create pollution.

According to the World Health Organization (WHO), over seven million people die each year because of air pollution. Polluted air harms plants and animals, too, creating a disastrous impact on the environment.

POLLUTION IN THE HOME

Most people think of pollution being in the air outside, but many suffer from pollution inside the home, too. The main source of inside pollution is cooking stoves that use fuel such as wood, kerosene, coal, or animal dung.

DID YOU KNOW? The WHO estimates that 99% of people breathe air that contains harmful pollutants.

Pollution and Industry

Before the Industrial Revolution, the world's population was small. Our planet could cope naturally with any pollution and waste that people made.

The Industrial Revolution

With the Industrial Revolution, people moved to cities and began working in factories. Cities became overcrowded and polluted with fumes from factory chimneys. Sewage and industrial waste were dumped into rivers. In the nineteenth century, many countries in Europe and North America built sewers that carried human waste and industrial pollution farther from sources of drinking water, but it still flooded into rivers and the sea.

The Industrial Revolution saw the rise in manufactured goods. Manufacturing is now spread all over the world. Consumerism (the desire to buy consumer goods) drives many of the environmental problems in the world, including pollution, carbon emissions, and using up resources.

With production and transportation technology, we produce far more than we actually need.

MACHINES AND FACTORIES

The Industrial Revolution began around 1760. As people discovered steam power, factories, train lines, and canals were all built, allowing products to be made and transported in greater and greater numbers.

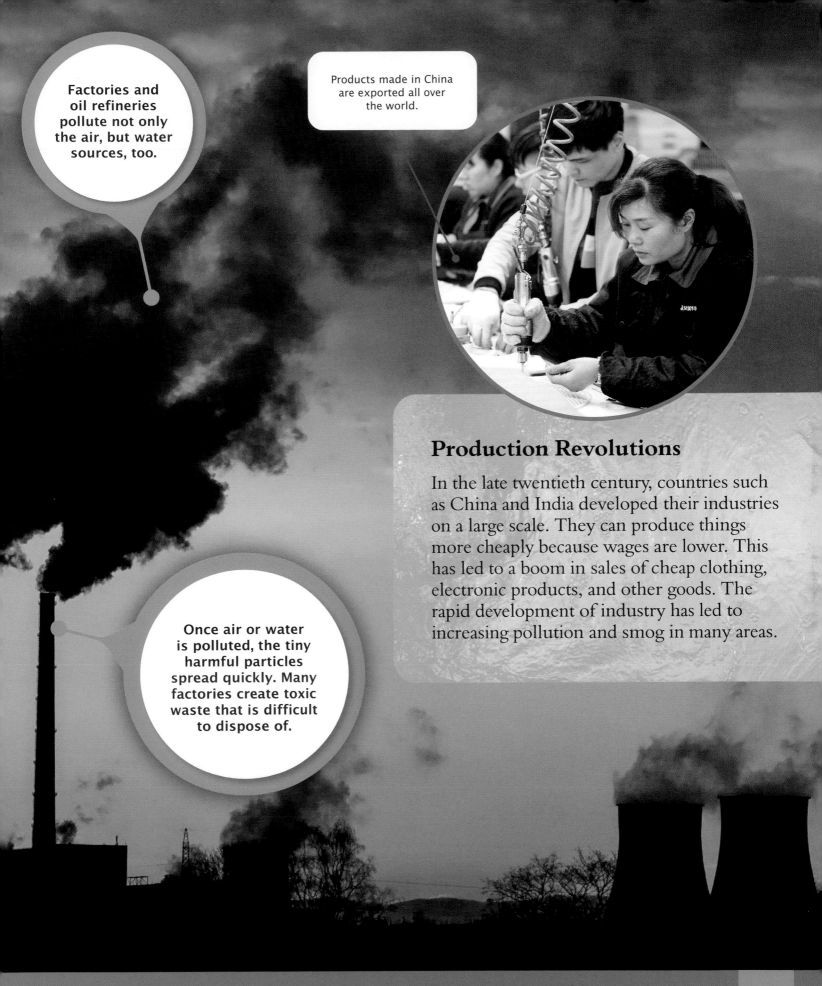

Factories and oil refineries pollute not only the air, but water sources, too.

Products made in China are exported all over the world.

Once air or water is polluted, the tiny harmful particles spread quickly. Many factories create toxic waste that is difficult to dispose of.

Production Revolutions

In the late twentieth century, countries such as China and India developed their industries on a large scale. They can produce things more cheaply because wages are lower. This has led to a boom in sales of cheap clothing, electronic products, and other goods. The rapid development of industry has led to increasing pollution and smog in many areas.

DID YOU KNOW? Soil can also be polluted by industrial waste, if waste is dumped and toxic chemicals leak into the ground.

Electronic Waste

Developments in science and technology have led to exciting gadgets that can improve our lives. However, there are now so many gadgets that they are causing environmental problems.

Most things we buy are wrapped in or made partly with plastic. Plastic can take thousands of years to decompose, and some of it never will.

Producing Gadgets and Devices

Most pollution caused by making gadgets comes from mining metals, including copper, gold, and chromium. Fossil fuels are burned to transport the metals to make devices in factories and when they are delivered to stores. Plastic packaging will be thrown into landfill sites as soon as phones and gadgets are bought.

Recycling used gadgets is difficult, so large amounts of electronic waste (e-waste) is sent to developing or low-income countries. Here, workers are not always protected when handling dangerous substances.

Billions of smartphones are in use around the world.

E-waste often ends up in landfill sites. Some is burned in incinerators, but this leaves toxic ash, which has to be buried in the ground.

REUSING AND RECYCLING

Nonrenewable precious metals are used when building gadgets and appliances. By throwing them away, we are throwing away valuable resources that we will not get back. Instead, they need to be reused or recycled.

Piling Up

Once they are thrown away, computers, televisions, game consoles, and smartphones can release toxic chemicals and metals, such as lead and mercury, into the environment. People replace some of these electrical items every couple of years, so the amount of pollution is building up.

Old electronic equipment causes mountains of waste and leads to pollution.

DID YOU KNOW? Medals from the 2020 Tokyo Olympic Games were made from metal taken from recycled consumer electronics.

77

The Air We Breathe

Around Earth is a thin blanket of gases. This blanket, or atmosphere, moves heat and water around the planet and is important to all life on Earth.

Producing Harmful Fumes

Air pollution is made up of gases, dust, and fumes that can harm people, plants, and animals. Most air pollution comes from burning fossil fuels and industrial processes.

Cars burn a mixture of air and gasoline (petrol), and this releases toxic gases, such as carbon monoxide, into the atmosphere as well as releasing carbon dioxide from the fuel. Car fumes mix with sunlight to form a poisonous brown haze called smog. Breathing in smog can cause lung and heart diseases.

Trees and plants can absorb (soak up) carbon dioxide. Unfortunately, we are releasing more carbon dioxide into the atmosphere than Earth's plants can absorb.

Traffic fumes are at their worst along our roads. The gases and particles in the fumes affect plants, animals, and people walking or cycling along the roads.

Iron is made in an iron foundry.

Making Metals

To make cars, trucks, trains, planes, and ships, we need metals such as iron and steel. Making metal in big factories, such as steel plants and iron foundries, releases particles of metals into the air as well as harmful gases.

DID YOU KNOW? Smog is a mix of the words "smoke" and "fog."

People need to walk along roads to get to work and schools. But the emissions they breathe in can cause very serious health problems.

CHILDREN AT RISK

Everyone can suffer from the effects of air pollution, but children are most at risk because their lungs are small and still developing. Also, since they are usually more active outdoors than adults, they breathe in a lot of air.

Unseen Dangers

Much pollution is invisible. We cannot see it even when it is harming the environment or our health. When dangerous materials are released into nature, they can have widespread effects on the planet that we don't see until it is too late.

Changing Our Ways

In the 1930s, people started using chemicals called CFCs to make household products such as aerosols and refrigerators. However, it was later discovered that these gases harmed the atmosphere, causing the ozone layer to become thin above the South and North Poles. In 1996, most industrial countries banned the use of CFCs. However, CFCs are still released into the air when old refrigerators and air-conditioning units are thrown away.

While tap water seems clean, it can still contain harmful substances, such as arsenic, copper, or lead. Water is easily polluted because so many things can dissolve in it. Waste from farms, factories, and towns all mix into water and pollute it.

Accidents at nuclear power plants can have long-term effects on the environment.

Nuclear Disaster

In 1986, an accident at the Chernobyl nuclear power plant in Ukraine sent a radioactive cloud over Western Europe. Wild areas of forest as well as farmland were poisoned by radioactive dust. The area around the old power plant will remain polluted and dangerous for thousands of years.

DID YOU KNOW? Light pollution can harm humans, too. It interrupts our bodies' natural processes and the release of chemicals that regulate them.

Part of our atmosphere is called the ozone layer. It protects life on Earth from harmful rays from the Sun.

Chemicals released into the air mix with water and fall to Earth as acid rain. This rain damages trees and enters the water systems

Ozone layer

Ozone in the atmosphere acts as a shield for Earth. Where it has become thin, more harmful UV light reaches Earth.

SEEN AND HEARD DANGERS

Light and noise pollution can harm the natural environment in the same way that chemicals can. Bright lights and loud noises can confuse birds and marine animals, leading them away from their natural habitats.

Getting Rid of Waste

With a world full of people using and throwing things away every day, waste has become a huge threat to the environment.

The Plastic Problem

Plastic is one of the most common materials used to make things. It is light, durable, and cheap to produce, but difficult to get rid of. Most countries use holes in the ground called landfill sites to dump their garbage. It slowly decays there, but it has not been dealt with, only hidden.

Although most plastic litter is thrown away on land, much of it ends up in the oceans. It is carried out to sea by rivers, wind, and tides. The rest comes from boats and ships. Plastic pollution kills seabirds, fish, and other marine animals.

Although there are systems in place to encourage recycling, we produce far more garbage than we can recycle. Often, developed nations ship waste to poorer countries, rather than dealing with it themselves.

Developed nations ship containers of waste to be recycled in other countries.

TIGHTER LAWS

In 2019, many nations signed an agreement to regulate how much plastic recycling is shipped abroad. Moving trash around for treatment uses fossil fuels, releasing carbon dioxide.

DID YOU KNOW? There is a drifting patch of plastic garbage in the Pacific Ocean that covers 1.6 million square km (610,000 square mi) of sea.

Piled Up

Where garbage is piled up rather than recycled, burned, or buried, it is easy for it to pollute air, water, and soil. Some blows away, some breaks down into tiny particles that are hard to deal with, and some releases dangerous gases as it decays.

Manila in the Philippines has seen huge garbage dumps develop because the government has not collected the waste.

On any beach in the world, you are likely to see plastic litter washed up by the waves.

Though plastic does not decompose completely, it does break down into microparticles. These are taken in by marine animals, and it causes them harm.

A Different Way

Many people are trying to live in ways that are less harmful to the environment. They change their homes and the way they travel to be more eco-friendly (kinder to the environment).

Starting at Home

Starting at home is a great way to make a difference. You might be able to change your energy supplier to one that uses clean energy, or think about how you could use less power by drying clothes outside and switching off electrical appliances you are not using. You might also be able to make more trips on foot or by bike, or use public transportation rather than a car.

Cutting our use of plastic is quite easy. If we stop using single-use plastic items, such as water bottles, throwaway cups, and wrappers, we can all make a difference.

People are starting to build ecohouses. These are designed to use less energy for running and heating.

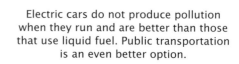

Electric cars do not produce pollution when they run and are better than those that use liquid fuel. Public transportation is an even better option.

REPLACING PLASTIC

Biodegradable plastics can replace some plastics made from oil. Many of these are made from plant sources. Properly treated, these will break down rather than stay in the environment causing problems for centuries.

Old shipping containers can be used to build houses, stores, restaurants, and even schools! Reuse is more ecofriendly than making new things.

DID YOU KNOW? Ecohomes can be built with grass roofs and tanks to collect rainwater.

What Is Poverty?

Many people are so poor that not even their basic needs are met. According to the United Nations (UN), more than 700 million people live in extreme poverty. With climate change, poverty will become worse.

Who Lives in Poverty?

Most people who live in extreme poverty are in Africa, Latin America, or Asia. Many of them lack even basic food, clothing, and shelter. Few have access to electricity, education, or health care.

> Poverty is a result of inequality. There is enough wealth in the world for everyone to live well, but it is not fairly shared out.

Even in wealthy countries, some people are very poor. Those who are worse off than most others in their society are living in what is called relative poverty. They include those with no jobs or low-paid work, as well as many elderly people. When people are poor, making eco-friendly choices is not an option. They struggle to meet basic needs however they can.

Providing education for all children is one of the aims of the UN.

From Poverty to Fairness

As people escape poverty, their better standard of living uses more resources. The environment is already under stress. Richer people will have to live more sustainable lives, so that we can all live well.

NATURE AND POVERTY

In many areas, environmental conditions lead to poverty. Droughts, floods, hurricanes, and other extreme weather events can destroy crops and homes. These problems will become worse and more widespread as the climate changes.

The International Poverty Line is set at $1.90 a day. People with less than this are classed as living in extreme poverty.

DID YOU KNOW? In 1981, 88% of Chinese people were counted as living in extreme poverty. Today, it is just 1%.

Rich and Poor

Poverty exists everywhere because people do not benefit equally from a country's wealth. There are also huge differences in wealth between nations.

How We Got Here

Over several centuries, European countries took raw materials, such as copper, from countries they had invaded and colonized in Africa, Asia, and South and Central America. At the same time, they prevented those countries from developing their own industries and infrastructure.

In the mid-twentieth century, most colonies gained freedom from foreign rule. It was hard for newly independent nations to compete in business with the richer industrialized countries. In some of these new nations, wars, corruption, and environmental problems have made poverty worse.

Although some low-income countries can borrow money, the interest on the loan puts the country in a lot of debt. This creates more problems.

The gap between rich and poor countries has been growing wider and wider.

CYCLES OF POVERTY

Societies in poor countries can find themselves in an endless cycle of poverty. A country in debt cannot afford schools, so people cannot be educated. Low education leads to poor work practices, which leads to low incomes.

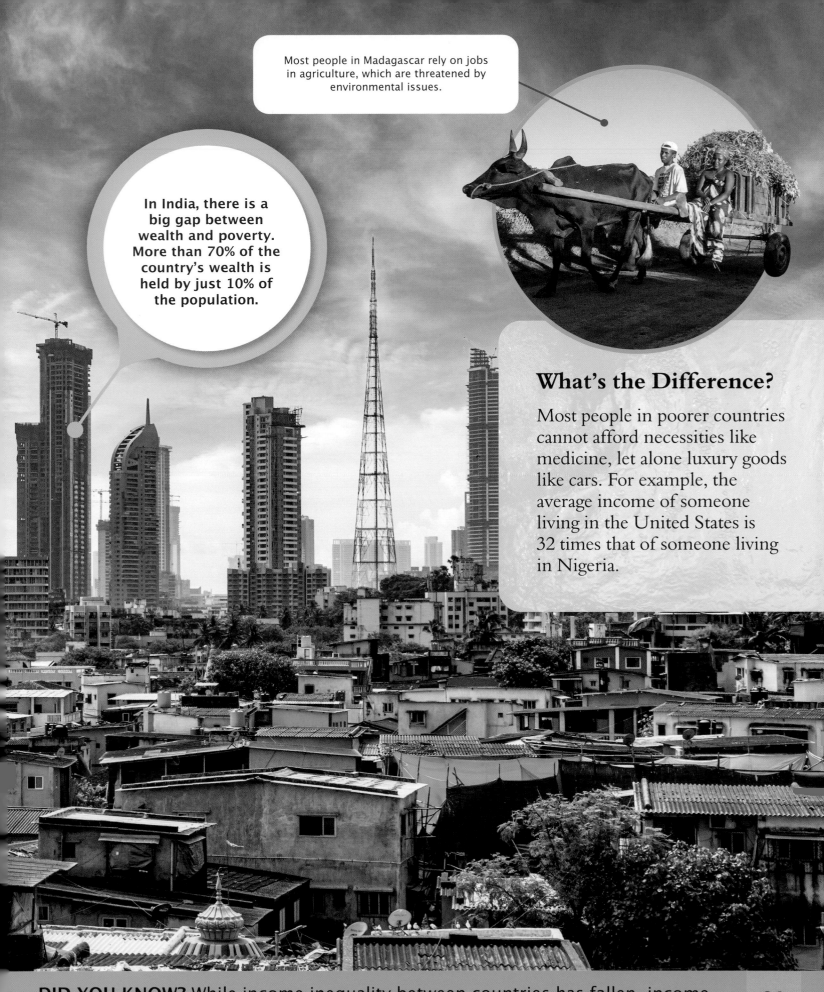

Most people in Madagascar rely on jobs in agriculture, which are threatened by environmental issues.

In India, there is a big gap between wealth and poverty. More than 70% of the country's wealth is held by just 10% of the population.

What's the Difference?

Most people in poorer countries cannot afford necessities like medicine, let alone luxury goods like cars. For example, the average income of someone living in the United States is 32 times that of someone living in Nigeria.

DID YOU KNOW? While income inequality between countries has fallen, income inequality within countries has risen.

Poverty and Water

The poorest people are most likely to get sick. Many of them live in slums or remote rural areas. One in three people—that's 2.2 billion people—do not have access to clean water. This will get worse in coming years.

Problems with Disease

In some slums, many people are forced to buy water at high prices from water sellers. With no waste collection or proper roads, there is mud and filth everywhere. The dirty conditions allow diseases to spread easily.

Contaminated, or dirty, drinking water can pass on diseases such as cholera, dysentery, typhoid, and polio. Diseases related to dirty water cause around 3.6 million deaths every year. With clean water, these deaths could be prevented.

Some people do not have running water at home. Many take water from rivers that may be contaminated. As water becomes more scarce in some areas, problems will become worse.

Clean Water

People need clean water, sanitation, and waste disposal to prevent diseases from spreading. Providing clean water for everyone is a priority, but this needs investment, particularly if it is to be achieved without damage to the environment. Poor countries cannot afford to make the investment alone.

Information about keeping water clean can save lives.

DID YOU KNOW? A report in 2017 showed that 3 billion people did not have a way to wash their hands with soap and water in their homes.

WATER IN AFRICA

The continent of Africa has the highest number of people without access to clean water. Why? A combination of a dry climate, limited systems for waste or water transportation, and climate change are all responsible.

Dirty drinking water is the cause of many serious diseases in poor countries.

Sewage runs through alleyways between poor housing.

Not Enough Food

In the world's poorest countries, nearly one person in every three does not get as much food as they need to give them the energy they require.

Going Hungry

Hunger has severe effects on health. For example, children who go hungry do not grow properly and are likely to suffer from health problems throughout their lives.

Meeting the UN's target to end food poverty by 2030 now looks unlikely. Climate change and wars cause problems for food systems. Areas that will be hit early by climate change already struggle to grow enough food.

Farming practices that damage the environment will make problems with food supplies worse. Degraded soil produces fewer crops, and polluted water and air reduce yields. Water scarcity makes it hard to farm.

Many poor people cannot grow enough food or do not have money to buy it. Governments distribute food to help the poorest.

Small-scale farming

Growing Food

In some countries, poor people can produce more food for themselves. One way forward is to introduce small-scale farming techniques that are suited to a specific local environment. Another way is to breed animals that require little food, such as poultry or farmed fish.

DID YOU KNOW? Researchers think that a healthy diet could improve food supplies. Less money spent on health care would mean that more could be spent on food.

Providing food supplies is a short-term solution to hunger. As environmental conditions become worse, it will be needed more often.

THE COVID-19 PANDEMIC

Food shortages for many were made worse by the global coronavirus pandemic in 2020 and 2021. Production and distribution of food were made more difficult for many people already suffering.

Getting an Education

Poorer people often receive less education. Without a good education, it is almost impossible for people to break out of poverty.

A Better Education

In many of the world's poorest countries, there are not enough schools or trained teachers. In many rural areas, there are more than 60 children in each class and few teaching materials, such as books.

In many countries, young children are not sent to school. Some children are kept home to work or do not have a school nearby. Children who live in war zones, or have fled from one, are often not able to go to school. As environmental changes force people to move around, their education will suffer further.

Many rural schools in Africa are short of basic equipment. Without funding, schools cannot be set up and run well.

Boys or Girls

Sometimes, poor families must choose whether to send a son or a daughter to school, and girls usually lose out. Boys are often chosen over girls because they will head the family and earn the most when they grow up.

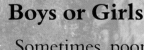

In some poorer countries, fewer girls than boys go to school.

Poor children often miss school because they have to work to help their families.

Education can help people understand threats to the environment and prepare for the changes that lie ahead.

HARD LESSONS

The impacts of damaging the environment and of climate change are not taught in all schools. Today's children are not being well prepared to live in a changed world.

DID YOU KNOW? During the Covid–19 pandemic, around 90% of students worldwide were out of the classroom.

Poverty and Resources

Most people in more economically developed countries (MEDCs) have good access to resources: food, water, shelter, and energy. Many living in less economically developed countries (LEDCs) have limited or no access.

Natural resources need to be sustainably managed, but this can happen only with investment in technology, education, and employment.

Difficult Decisions

Some poor countries are rich in natural resources, which they sell to other countries. Many resources are also mined by companies from outside the country, so the profits go elsewhere.

Mining natural resources causes environmental problems, such as pollution and desertification. This harms natural habitats and farmland. The damage worsens, while the benefit of the resources goes to the rich countries that buy them. People in richer countries rarely see the harm that has been caused by what they buy.

People in poor countries often use their natural resources to make things to sell to rich countries. When resources run out, they have nothing left.

NATURAL DISASTERS

Many developing nations are at risk from climate change and the natural disasters it brings. They are more vulnerable because they do not have the money to build structures that will be safe from disasters. It costs a lot of money to rebuild after a disaster.

New Solutions

Ethiopia is a landlocked country in Africa. Around 67% of the population work in farming, but many still do not have enough to eat. Droughts, poor access to markets, and lack of training and equipment make life difficult for farmers. Training helps farmers learn new techniques and conservation skills, which allow them to protect their environment and grow more.

Farmers can produce excellent crops by adding compost to the soil.

New ways of watering land are helping to save water and grow better crops. Saving water will help farmers survive in a hotter, drier world.

DID YOU KNOW? A developing country is one that has low–level industrial development that leads to social and economic problems.

97

More Aid Needed

Aid can help people during emergencies and can help rebuild their communities afterward. As the impact of climate change increases, more people will need help.

Foreign Aid

For 20 years, extreme poverty had been declining around the world. Then, following the Covid-19 pandemic, another 100 million people were put into poverty, and poverty levels rose again.

Since 1970, the UN has encouraged developed countries to spend 0.7% of their annual income as aid. Aid funds can be used both for development and to help in emergencies. The need for aid will increase as the impact of climate change is felt, but it can also be used to help poorer countries meet environmental goals. To protect our planet, all countries need sustainable sources of food, water, and energy.

Environmental damage will increase the call for aid, as more natural disasters leave people in need.

Reducing Aid

Countries around the world have been so hard hit by the Covid-19 pandemic that they have reduced the amount of money they give to foreign aid. This means that education, health, food, and countless other initiatives supported by developed nations will suffer until these economies start to recover.

DID YOU KNOW? Ending poverty is the number one goal of the United Nations' 17 sustainable development goals.

International help to provide a clean water supply or renewable power sources can help build a sustainable future.

It is important that aid is used to help people develop sustainable ways of living, avoiding the mistakes of developed countries.

UNITED NATIONS

The United Nations is an international organization set up after World War II. It coordinates aid and other initiatives to try and end poverty, need, and suffering around the world.

Too Much Waste

Humans create millions of tons of waste every day. We need to produce less to protect the planet.

What Is Waste?

Hundreds of years ago, people produced very little waste. Most waste, such as food, wood, and ash from fires, was biodegradable. This means that it would rot away and become part of the soil again. Today, a lot of our waste does not break down, and the piles of garbage keep growing.

> Some materials, such as plastics and polythene, take thousands of years to break down.

Our factories produce large quantities of synthetic materials, such as nylon and plastic. Consumer products, such as microwave ovens, televisions, computers, and smartphones, contain materials that will never fully break down. These items are made using valuable resources that should not be wasted.

Materials that do not break down can be carried long distances by the sea and winds. There are ways to dispose of waste properly. Dumping rubbish in landfill sites is the easiest option, but it is bad for the environment.

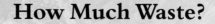

How Much Waste?

In 2019, the world's people produced 1.8 billion tonnes (2 billion tons) of waste. By 2050, we are expected to produce 3 billion tonnes (3.4 billion tons) each year.

WASTING WASTE

Much waste goes unsorted, so materials that could be reused or recycled are thrown away along with waste that is truly useless.

Litter is a common sight everywhere around the planet.

Developed nations produce far more waste than developing nations, because they use more of the world's resources.

DID YOU KNOW? One of the biggest landfill sites is in the USA. It covers more than 8.9 square km (3.4 square mi)!

Landfill Sites

Most of the waste that is produced goes into landfill sites. What is dumped varies around the world, but it is usually a mix of household and commercial waste.

Piling Up

Landfills are built into or on top of the ground to store and bury waste. The garbage in a landfill site is squashed and covered up with a layer of soil each day to prevent it from smelling or blowing away.

Modern landfills are designed to prevent chemicals from leaking into the soil. At some landfills, methane gas is collected and then sold as fuel, or burned to generate electricity. This is not the case all around the world. Many landfill sites are hazards that cause pollution and harm people and wildlife. Even well-managed landfill sites store up problems for the future with waste that never rots.

Chemicals and oil can seep out of old landfill sites.

Contamination

Years ago, landfill sites were built without any thought of pollution. Today, even though they are built with special liners to prevent leaks, some leaking will happen over time. Sites need to be constantly monitored, so that groundwater sources are not contaminated.

DID YOU KNOW? The first landfill sites were in Crete in 3,000 BCE!

Every day, landfill sites get more full as more garbage is brought in.

Landfills produce harmful gases such as methane and carbon dioxide.

DISASTERS IN WAITING

Climate change is shifting weather patterns and leading to more extreme storms and flooding. Sites that hold landfill are being eroded, which increases the risk of rivers and other water systems becoming polluted.

Burning Waste for Energy

To try and solve both the waste and energy crises, some countries have started burning waste to create energy. There are both benefits and disadvantages to this plan.

How It Works

Different types of waste can be burned, such as plastics and chemical substances. Modern incinerators can recover the heat generated and produce electricity with it. The high temperatures can destroy the dangerous toxins and substances in some waste, so this system can be better than using landfill.

The first incinerators pumped gases straight into the air, causing pollution. Modern incinerators clean the smoke produced before releasing it, so that only clean air is released. However, many old incinerator plants are still in use.

Burning waste takes up less space than landfills. But it also produces waste gases, such as carbon dioxide.

Rubber can be recycled

CHANGING FROM COAL

It may be possible to change old coal power plants into waste-to-energy power plants. It is expensive, but it would avoid having to knock down power plants and continue to provide jobs in the local area.

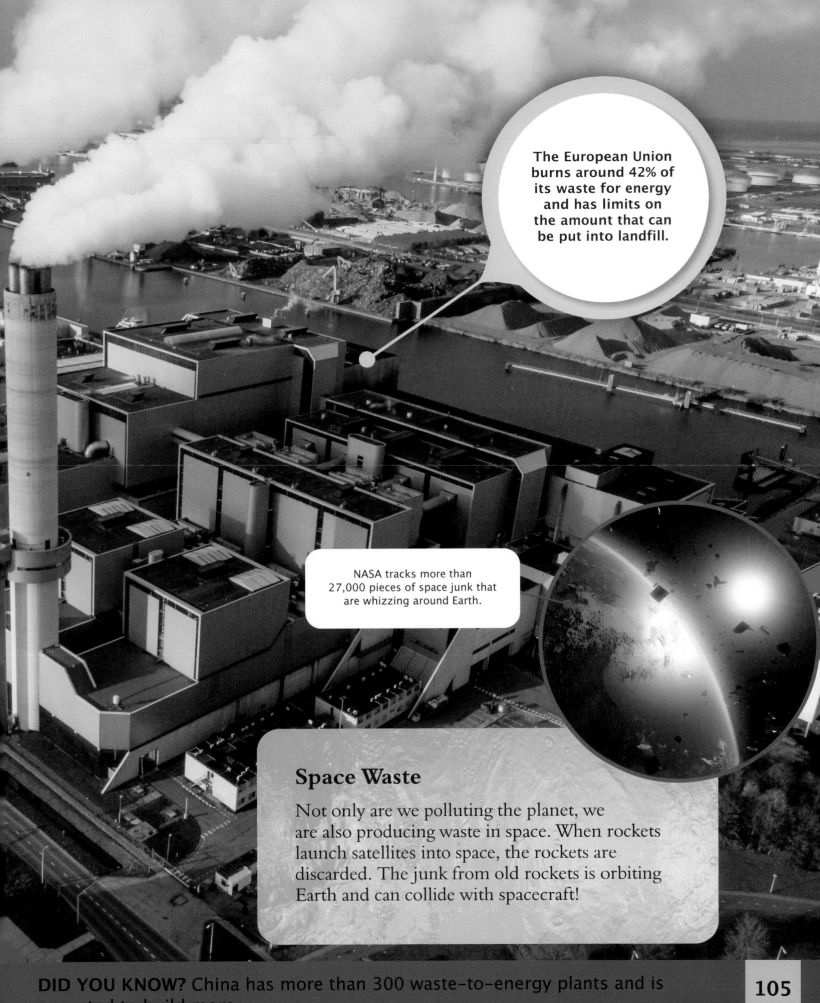

The European Union burns around 42% of its waste for energy and has limits on the amount that can be put into landfill.

NASA tracks more than 27,000 pieces of space junk that are whizzing around Earth.

Space Waste

Not only are we polluting the planet, we are also producing waste in space. When rockets launch satellites into space, the rockets are discarded. The junk from old rockets is orbiting Earth and can collide with spacecraft!

DID YOU KNOW? China has more than 300 waste-to-energy plants and is expected to build more.

Sending Waste Abroad

There are strict health and safety regulations when recycling toxic waste, and it is very expensive. Companies and governments send much of their waste to countries with fewer regulations and cheaper workforces.

Much scrap metal is exported to nations that are better able to process it.

Where Does It Go?

Before 2018, vast amounts of recycling waste were exported from nations such as the UK, United States, Canada, and Ireland to China. The Chinese government became increasingly concerned about pollution and banned imports of most of the waste. Much waste was then sent to Malaysia, Turkey, Poland, and Indonesia. However, in 2021, Malaysian authorities started to push back against becoming the world's dumping ground.

Far more recycling is produced than can be recycled. It ends up being stored badly or outside, and this means that it degrades and cannot then be recycled.

Pollution in Indian recycling villages causes many people to develop breathing problems.

Health Problems

Poor countries often import waste to generate income. But their people are often not protected from the harmful effects of dealing with the waste.

DIRTY WASTE

Much of the waste that is exported is not clean enough to be recycled. If it is too contaminated to be sorted and recycled, it has to go to landfill, which causes environmental problems.

Plastic is the biggest contributor to exported waste, but metal and paper are also sent overseas.

DID YOU KNOW? The USA produces 14 million tonnes (15 million tons) of used clothes each year. Of that, 15% is sent for recycling, usually in India.

A World of Products

As our standards of living improve, we produce more waste. Disposable goods such as pens, toothbrushes, and batteries have become part of our lives.

Spend, Spend, Spend

Every year, people throw away 80 billion pairs of disposable wooden chopsticks, using up 2 million trees. People in developed countries replace their smartphones on average every 18 months, even though a phone could last up to eight years.

Today, we have moved a long way from shopping for what we need. We buy more food than we need to live. We buy products for fun and to make our lives easier, rather than because we need them. We buy clothes so that we can choose what to wear each day, rather than only what we need.

While it is normal to want new things, consumerism is now out of control. Targeted advertising tracks people's spending habits and interests and sends them advertisements for things they might want to buy. This can make people feel as though they need new things, even though they don't.

Constantly buying new things creates a lot of waste and uses valuable resources.

SWAP SINGLE USE

Single-use items are a big source of waste. A plastic bottle of water is used only once before being thrown away. Instead, you could choose a reusable bottle. Towns can help by installing fountains where water bottles can be refilled.

Doing, Not Buying

While it can feel like buying new things will make us happy, the buzz we feel is very short-lived. Studies have shown that our money would be better spent on experiences that will have a longer-lasting impact on us. This might be saving for a special outing or meeting friends to see a show.

Some people are trying to counter out-of-control spending by promoting no-spending days, giving days, and creative schemes for making things.

We need to think about what we actually need before deciding to buy. It also helps to think about what will happen to your old things when you buy new ones.

DID YOU KNOW? There are now more mobile (cell) phones in the world than there are people.

109

Reducing Waste

The best solution to the waste problem is to reduce the amount of waste we create. Changes in the way we buy and use products will help.

Ways to Change

You should always ask yourself if something has to be thrown away. Your friends or family may want your used items. Or you could donate them to a charity or sell them in a garage sale or on the Internet.

If we stop buying goods that have lots of packaging, companies will have to rethink how they package their products. Always take your own shopping bag, so you don't need to use a disposable plastic bag. We can also look for products that are made from recycled materials.

We can reduce waste by not buying overpackaged goods and things we don't really need.

Reusing textiles is now a major industry.

Fast Fashion

Over the past 20 years, clothes have become cheaper and cheaper. They are often produced by people working in terrible conditions for very little money. They are a source of greenhouse gas production, water and air pollution, and enormous amounts of waste. Today, there is a drive toward sustainable fashion. Clothes should be repaired, resold, or recycled. Synthetic fabrics can be replaced with natural ones; even fish skin and pineapple plants can be used to create fabrics.

DID YOU KNOW? The Japanese village of Kamikatsu recycles 80% of its waste into 45 categories!

Thinking about how we shop, eat, work, and travel can all contribute to reducing waste.

Old books, toys, and clothes can be donated to charities.

TOYS

REDUCE REUSE RECYCLE

With so many countries struggling with the amount of waste produced, the best thing we can do is to REDUCE the amount we buy, REUSE items instead of throwing them away, and RECYCLE as much as we can.

A World of Water

Water is necessary for almost all life on Earth. Humans can go many days without food, but without water we could die in just 48 hours.

Water Everywhere!

Water covers around 71% of Earth's surface. Most of Earth's water is salt water, which humans and other animals cannot drink. This is contained in the world's oceans.

Just 2.5% of water is fresh water. This is found in lakes, rivers, streams, frozen in ice and glaciers, and underground. The water we use for drinking, washing, and growing food comes from rainwater, lakes, and underground water sources.

Most fresh water is trapped in ice or as groundwater deep below Earth's surface.

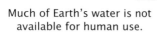

Much of Earth's water is not available for human use.

We Need Water

Water makes up around 70% of the human body. Without it, our bodies simply fail. Most other living things on our planet also contain large amounts of water. Desert plants and animals can live in extremely dry conditions but need some water in order to survive.

DID YOU KNOW? Seawater has different amounts of salt in it. The saltiest seawater is in a small lake in Antarctica called Don Juan Pond.

From space, it is easy to see that our planet is mostly covered by water.

Seas and lakes can be very deep. The Pacific, Atlantic, and Indian Oceans are around 4 km (2.4 mi) deep.

THE WATER CYCLE

The world's water follows a continuous cycle: Water evaporates from oceans and lakes, it forms clouds in the sky, and it falls as rain. The rain seeps into the ground, and forms rivers that run into lakes and oceans.

Who Has the Water?

Water available for human use is in short supply. It is also spread unevenly across the world.

Most and Least

The regions of South and North America have the most renewable fresh water. Northern Africa, Central Asia, and the Middle East have the least fresh water.

Around 4 billion people live in places where water is scarce. Water scarcity means that water does not reach the people who need it. Countries in sub-Saharan Africa have some of the worst water shortages.

Countries in North Africa, the Middle East, and South Asia have high levels of water stress. They use more water than their natural resources allow. Most of it is used for agriculture, but much of the produce they grow is exported.

While some regions have always had much less water than others, climate change, pollution, and pressure on agriculture have made the situation worse for many countries.

Water in Asia

Asia has the highest amount of available water. But Asia also has a huge population. Poor water treatment is leading to high levels of water pollution from human waste, agriculture, and industry, which is making this valuable resource even more stressed.

The amount of usable water available for each person is what really matters.

DID YOU KNOW? One in four people do not have access to safe drinking water.

Natural disasters, such as storms and floods, can make problems with water supplies worse.

More than half the world's people have trouble finding enough water.

PRESSURE ON WATER

Enormous amounts of water are needed for agriculture. With a rising world population, there will be pressure on farmers to produce more food. This will put more stress on water sources.

The Importance of Aquifers

One way to source water is to drill for groundwater stored in aquifers. These are natural underground water stores.

Sinking Cities

Some aquifers are vast and ancient. One example is the Ogallala Aquifer in the United States. At 10,000 years old, this 450,000 square km (174,000 square mi) underground reservoir supplies huge amounts of water for drinking and agriculture in the central United States. However, parts of it are now starting to run dry.

In some places, so much water has been taken out of the ground that the surface is sinking. This has happened in California where the ground settled 8.5 m (28 ft) over 50 years. This is a problem for many cities, including Tehran in Iran and Jakarta in Indonesia. Aquifers are also threatened by pollution from pesticides and chemicals that seep into the ground.

Aquifers are the main source of water for many large cities.

Deep wells take water from aquifers in dry regions.

DID YOU KNOW? Fresh water that has collected underground over thousands of years is known as "fossil water."

Wells and Boreholes

Remote rural areas often depend on wells and small boreholes that connect to underground water supplies. Without them, people are vulnerable to diseases spread by dirty water. As more water is drawn from underground for drinking, cooking, and farming, supplies dry up. The ground becomes too dry for plants to grow, and even more water is needed for agriculture.

Small wells and boreholes provide water for many people.

Centuries of pumping water from the aquifer under Mexico City has caused it to sink dramatically.

WILL IT REFILL?

Aquifers are rock or sediment soaked with water. The water can be extracted by drilling or digging a well. An aquifer refills slowly as water sinks through the ground into it. If we use groundwater from aquifers too quickly, they will not have time to refill.

Shrinking Rivers and Lakes

In our search for water, we have caused rivers to run dry and lakes to dry up. The effects include loss of habitats and increased air pollution.

Drying Up

Huge amounts of water are taken from river systems to irrigate (water) crops. In the United States, water is taken from the Colorado River to water crops fed to cattle raised for beef and dairy products. Growing crops that people could eat directly would be a more efficient use of water. So much water has been taken, that the river does not now reach the sea.

As rivers dry up, sand and silt are no longer deposited (laid down) at the river mouth. These deposits protected the land from ocean waves. Without them, salt water can flow inland, destroying local habitats and wildlife that are unable to cope with the high salt levels.

Lakes are fed by rivers. Changing snowmelt from mountains and increased use of river water for farming means that less reaches the lakes.

The drying up of the Aral Sea has caused many problems for wildlife and people.

Aral Sea Disaster

The Aral Sea in central Asia was once the world's fourth-biggest lake. In the 1960s, the waters feeding it were diverted for irrigating cotton fields. Now, the Aral Sea is only one-tenth of its former size, and lake and river ecosystems have been destroyed. The dry ground where the sea once was turns to poisonous dust and causes health problems for the local people.

CROSSING BORDERS

It is often hard to protect rivers that flow across many different countries. If a river runs through a protected area in one country, it may still be affected by actions farther up or downstream.

Global warming means that more water is evaporating, and lake water levels are falling. This harms ecosystems in the lake and nearby communities.

When rivers fail to reach the sea, the coasts erode faster.

DID YOU KNOW? Only one-third of the rivers in the world are free-flowing, without any human interventions, such as dams.

119

Dam Dangers

People have been building dams for thousands of years as a way of capturing water to use. Dams allow water to be stored, flooding to be controlled, and they can produce power.

Good and Bad

In the past, dams were small and had little impact on natural environments. At the start of the twentieth century, there were only a few hundred large dams. During the twentieth century, however, dams became bigger and more widespread. By 2019, there were more than 60,000.

While dams are a good way to store water and they can prevent flooding, there are negative effects, too. Blocking the flow of river water transforms underwater habitats, destroying the homes of many aquatic species. This also destroys the communities that depend on them. Campaigners against dams argue that people should use water more efficiently instead of building dams.

Flooding Villages

When a dam is built, the area above the dam is flooded, destroying natural habitats. If people live on this land, they must be relocated to another place. Around 80 million people have been displaced because of dam building.

The reservoirs created by large dams mean that whole towns are sometimes flooded.

DID YOU KNOW? China's Three Gorges Dam is the world's biggest hydropower dam. The project displaced more than 1.2 million people.

Hydroelectric dams produce power as water flows through giant turbines inside them.

Reservoirs of water collect behind dams. This can be used to provide water to households, industry, and agriculture.

Many dams are built to produce hydropower. While this energy is renewable, some campaigners argue that it is damaging to the environment.

REMOVING DAMS

In some places, dams are now being removed to restore natural ecosystems. Two hydroelectric dams on the Elwha River in Washington, USA, were removed between 2011 and 2014, and the river ecosystem is recovering.

Water on a Warmer Planet

Scientists are working hard to predict the effects of climate change and global warming. What will happen to the water cycle, and how can we cope with the changes?

Floods and Droughts

In many parts of the world, too much rainfall has caused floods and destroyed natural habitats, homes, and crops. In others, rainfall has decreased, causing droughts. One of the biggest effects of global warming is the melting of the polar ice caps. As more meltwater reaches the oceans, sea levels rise.

Coastal cities are at great risk of flooding if sea levels rise. They may also lose their supplies of fresh water, if salt water seeps into groundwater reserves. Salt in the ground makes land unusable for farming, because crops will not grow.

Flooded Farmland

Large, well-populated areas of farmland, such as the Nile and Ganges river deltas, are at risk of being submerged under seawater. New areas of irrigated farmland would have to be created to take the place of lost coastal farmland.

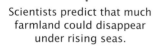

Scientists predict that much farmland could disappear under rising seas.

DID YOU KNOW? The sea level will continue to rise for some time, but if people reduce their emissions to combat global heating, the rise can be limited.

Melting glaciers and ice sheets are a sign of global heating.

Many of the world's coastal cities, like Venice in Italy, will experience worse floods with climate change.

When high spring tides combine with strong winds, the water levels rise, and Venice floods. Many ancient landmarks are damaged, along with homes and infrastructure.

WARMING THE WATER CYCLE

As the planet warms, water will evaporate more quickly. This increased evaporation will lead to more frequent, heavy rainfalls.

The Value of Water

Most of us are very wasteful with water. Water is wasted in homes, in industries, on farms, in yards and gardens, and even by those who supply it.

Wasting Water

Tap water is very cheap. For example, bottled water costs around 500 times more than water that is piped into homes. Some countries use water meters, and people pay for the amount of water they use. This helps them to be more careful with their water use.

In poor countries, women and children may travel every day to collect water. Their journeys can be more than 6 km (4 mi) long and take several hours. They often share water sources with domestic and wild animals. When such effort is needed to obtain water, people use it very carefully.

Leaving water running is a simple waste of water that can easily be prevented.

WAYS TO CHANGE

In the future, individuals, communities, and governments will all need to think about using less water. This might change the garden plants you have, the clothes you buy, or the crops that farmers grow.

Turning the water off while brushing your teeth is a good way to reduce the amount you use and maybe money, too.

If water pipes are not maintained, they will leak and waste water.

There are lots of ways to save water at home. Taking a shorter shower is a good place to start!

Leaking Pipes

Water companies and governments also need to improve efficiency. In the United States, up to 30% of the nation's water supply is lost through leaking pipes before it reaches homes and businesses.

DID YOU KNOW? The United States, China, and India use the most household water each year.

Glossary

AGRICULTURE The practice of farming, including raising animals and growing crops.

ALLERGY A sensitivity to a particular food or other substance that causes the body to react. Allergic reactions can be dangerous.

ATMOSPHERE The layer of gases that surround Earth or another planet.

ATOM The smallest possible part of something; it cannot be seen with the naked eye.

BIODEGRADABLE Able to break down naturally.

BIODIVERSITY The mix of plants and animals that are in one region.

CLIMATE The weather in a place over a period of time.

CONSUMERISM The trend in society for buying more and more goods.

CONTAMINATED Made unclean or polluted, possibly by harmful substances.

DEVELOPED COUNTRIES Countries that are advanced industrially, economically, and socially.

DEVELOPING COUNTRIES Countries that are poor and that are less advanced economically and socially than developed countries.

ECONOMY The supply of money and production of goods and services in a region or country.

ECOSYSTEM All the organisms that work together to live in a particular region.

ELEMENT A chemical that cannot be broken down into other substances, a pure substance.

EMISSIONS The gases given out by a process, such as running a car engine.

ENERGY The power needed to do a particular task.

ERODE To wear away.

EXPORTS The goods one country sells to another.

EXTINCT To be no longer living, so that there are no more of a species left in the world.

GENETICALLY MODIFIED Adapted by changing the genetic information, so that any organism behaves or grows in a different way.

GOVERNMENT The group of people who control and regulate a country.

HABITAT An animal's natural living environment.

HYDROELECTRICITY Electricity generated using fast-flowing water.

IMPORTS The goods that are bought and brought into one country from another.

INDUSTRY The activity that involves making raw materials into products, usually in factories.

INFRASTRUCTURE The systems, such as road, water, and power networks, usually needed for a society to work.

INTERVENTION The action of becoming involved in something to change the outcome.

IRRIGATION The supply of water to crops, usually created by people.

KEROSENE A fuel oil that comes from petroleum.

LIVELIHOOD A person's means of gaining the income to support themselves.

MICROORGANISM A super-small organism, such as a bacterium.

MIGRATE To move from one region to another. A migrant is a person who moves from one place to another; an immigrant is a person who moves permanently to live in another country.

MOLECULES Two or more atoms joined together.

NUTRIENTS The substances that all organisms need to grow and live.

POISONOUS Containing substances that will cause harm, illness, or death if taken into the body.

PREDATOR An animal that preys on (hunts) other animals.

RADIOACTIVE Relates to a substance that gives out harmful energy.

RECYCLE To break something down and use the material to produce a new item.

RESOURCES Supplies of essentials, such as food and water, that help people live. Natural resources are those that come from Earth.

SEWAGE Wastewater and human waste, usually transported through sewers.

SPECIES A specific type of organism; one organism can breed with another of the same species.

SUSTAINABLE Able to be used without using up or harming natural resources.

TROPICS The area of Earth just above and just below the equator.

WELFARE The health and well-being of people or animals.

WORKFORCE The people working in a country or for a particular business or organization.

Index